PLANETARY CYCLES

PLANETARY CYCLES

Astrological Indicators of Crises & Change

BETTY LUNDSTED

Samuel Weiser, Inc.

York Beach, Maine

First published in 1984 by
Samuel Weiser, Inc.
Box 612
York Beach, ME 03910

Reprinted 1986

ISBN 0-87728-630-2

Library of Congress Card Number: 84-51107

Typeset in 10 point Baskerville by
Positive Type, Millerton, NY

Manufactured in the United States of America by
Mitchell-Shear, Inc.

CONTENTS

Preface xi

Part 1: Planetary Cycles and How They Work 1

Part 2: Crisis Years: Ages and Stages 83

Part 3: Counseling a Crisis 137

Appendix: More Cycles 165

This book is dedicated to the
memory of
Samuel Weiser
for he made it possible
for many of us to find the path.

Acknowledgments

In this cycle in my life, it's important to me to thank everyone who helped me on my way during my study of astrology. First I want to thank Mr. Willis, wherever he may be, for he read my chart many years ago, and by doing so, opened up a whole new possibility of existence for me. His insight helped me to understand myself, and was the basis for my subsequent interest in the study of astrology. I appreciate my teachers, for each had something special to offer: Zoltan Mason got me started on the path when astrology classes were hard to find in New York City; Lynne Palmer taught her wonderful marathon classes on the West Side; Lionel Day combined metaphysics with the study of the person in the chart. Because of my previous study of psychology, philosophy, mythology and religion, my interest in astrology was primarily concerned with using astrology as a therapeutic tool. Lionel Day taught astrology with a special emphasis on psychological motivation, offering a degree program at the Astrosophical Institute, and although I did not pursue a degree from his school, I thoroughly enjoyed my years of study with his organization.

I also want to thank the American Federation of Astrologers for existing, for as a result of membership, I learned that there were many different kinds of astrologers in this country, each specializing in a particular branch of the field. By reading AFA journals, I learned about conferences in my area, and attended several. By going to conferences, I could expand my horizons and change my perspective.

Going to conferences somehow sparked a meeting with Charles Emerson, and I want to thank you, Charles, for believing in me. Because of Charles, I joined the National Council for Geocosmic

Research in New York. Because of Charles, I became involved with the education program for the New York Chapter of the NCGR. As a result of joining the NCGR, and eventually becoming a member of the national board, I had a chance to meet and talk with astrologers from all over the country while planning and administrating seminars and conferences for the education program.

This contact with the world of astrology taught me one very important thing: no one has a "special" astrology. If we decide to specialize in understanding human motivation, and how that manifests in a natal chart, the chances are we will. Astrologers who use different methods than mine, and work with different aspect structures than mine, will still come to similar conclusions about the chart being discussed. We are a part of a very special group, and by working together we are able to share information with each other, and this sharing results in developing maximum potential. This concept was reinforced again in a New York Group that formed to explore the combination of astrology and psychology. Thanks go to Dr. Bernard Rosenblum for hosting that group.

To astrologers, wherever you are in this country, my thanks to all of you for making our world better. To the authors who gave us books to read, thank you. And to the many unsung teachers who have worked for years to teach us all, a special thank you, for you are the foundation that the astrological community builds upon today. Prior to 1970, teachers and books were hard to find. Thank you for laying the groundwork for an environment where anyone can study astrology with ease.

To Neil Michelsen, who published my first book; to Marsha Kaplan Rie for believing I could do it; to Patricia Morimando who believed I could finish it—a special and personal kind of thanks. Special thanks go to Pat for rewriting my first book, and for editing this one, and most of all, for giving the counsel that only a friend can.

Thanks to another special group of people, for you gave me help in a personal way when I needed it most. Without your help, this book would not have been finished: Nancy Hastings, Doris Hebel, Carole Jones, Peter Jones, Barbara Somerfield, Mary Vohryzek, and Donald Wharton.

PREFACE

This book is about cycles and how they relate to the maturation process. Although various kinds of cycles have interested astrologers for centuries, my interest in cycles began when I heard a lecture given by Lionel Day in 1971. He discussed astrological cycles as indicators of personal growth, and this was the first time I heard about Saturn or Uranus being used as indicators of cyclic change rather than being considered just transits. Soon afterward, a friend gave me a copy of Grant Lewi's *Astrology for the Millions*, and I read Lewi's discussion of the changes that take place when Saturn, for instance, wends its cyclic way around the natal chart. Several years later, John Townley delivered a lecture on cycles for the National Council for Geocosmic Research in New York City; after hearing his lecture, I read his book *Astrological Cycles and The Life Crisis Periods*. To round out my studies, *The Practice of Astrology* by Dane Rudhyar was reissued, being a reprint of previously published articles that appeared in *Horoscope* in the 1940s. Alexander Ruperti's *Cycles of Becoming* was published in 1978, and cycles are also discussed in *Life Clock*, Volume 1, by Bruno and Louise Huber, adding to the information available to the contemporary astrologer.

My effort to explain cycles differs from previously published material in that it attempts to show, in simple terms, how the cycles work when we are trying to get from Monday to Tuesday. It has been written as a companion to *Transits: The Time of Your Life*, and should have been published in 1980, right after *Transits* came out. It was delayed because of my own experience with midlife crisis; because of that experience, this is probably a better book than it would have been if it was published earlier.

To completely explore the concept of cycles, the material has been divided into three parts. First we'll look at all the astrological cycles, moving from minor cycles (Sun, Moon, Mercury and Venus), to what we'll call maturation cycles (or the energy symbolized by cycles of Mars, Jupiter and Saturn). We end with the cycles of individuation* that are indicated by the various phases in the cycles of Uranus, Neptune, and Pluto. This section also includes information about aspects, orbs, how retrograde motion works in relation to cycles, and tables which show the average movement of the planets in their cycles during the course of a lifetime.

Part 2 is an exploration of ages and stages of growth, and indicates how cyclic phases manifest in combination during crisis years. These crisis years are normal stress periods for any human being. Some crisis years are familiar, and some are just beginning to be considered important to the process of maturation in our present day society. Part 3 is a discussion of a sample chart, so students can see how cyclic energy can be combined with other predictive techniques when conducting a session with a client.

As you will see, the cycles have not been continued in any depth past the age of eighty-four. Although I'm familiar with some of the material available about the maturation process of a lifetime, I consider myself a novice. This book has been written as a result of personal study, teaching a cycles class for a number of years, and the wonderful response from my clients. I feel that a lot more could be done with cycles as they relate to our older years than I have been able to do here. If any reader wishes to share personal experience with phases in Jupiter or Saturn cycles after the age of fifty-six, I would really enjoy hearing about it. Please write to me in care of the publisher and the correspondence will be forwarded.

---

*The individuation process referred to in this book is based on Jung's concept of integrating "conscious" with "unconscious" so the individual actually experiences the process of differentiation—the goal being the development of an individual personality. Most people imitate others rather than risking this process. With individuation also comes a need to be part of the universal collective. Individuation should not be confused with isolationism, or the selfish individualistic behavior associated with egocentricity.

PLANETARY CYCLES

Part 1

PLANETARY CYCLES
AND HOW THEY WORK

All the world's a stage
And all the men and women merely players:
They all have their exits and their entrances;
And one man in his time plays many parts...
                                    As You Like It
                                    Act 2, Scene 7

Shakespeare talked about stages of life many years ago. We play infant, youth, warrior, mother, father, grandparent, wise old man or woman. It doesn't matter if we are prepared to play our roles or not, for we play them anyway, and our various roles in life can be associated with the maturation process. Some years ago, Dane Rudhyar mentioned that one cycle of Uranus (or 84 years) could be considered the indication of a complete lifetime.[1] He said that Uranian energy relates to three major crises in life: coming of age at 21, the psychological crisis that happens about age 42, and the age of philosophy at 63 which pushes us toward either the development of the spiritual seed or senility. He called these critical ages "challenges to metamorphosis" because the challenge is offered so we can transcend the norm. If we understand these Uranian challenges ahead of time, and if we also work with the phases of other planetary cycles along the way, we will be better prepared to cope with our development.

This part of the book is devoted to a discussion of cycles from an astrological viewpoint. Each planet has a cycle of its own, and the cycle can be timed according to the planet's placement in the birth chart. Some cycles are more important than others, for the Sun completes one cycle a year, while Saturn completes one cycle every 28 years. We will look at cycles in terms of the planets and the different time sequence associated with each one. We shall work with approximate (or average) orbits for the planets to make the material easy to understand, but the reader should keep in mind that

[1]Dane Rudhyar, *The Practice of Astrology*, Sevire, Wassenaar, Holland, 1968, pp. 114. Most of this book is reprinted from articles that appeared in *Horoscope* between 1945 and 1946.

Table 1. Approximate Crisis Years*†

Age	Jupiter	Saturn	Uranus	Neptune	Pluto
3	xxx				
6	xxx				
7		xxx			
9	xxx				
12	xxx				
14		xxx			
15	xxx				
18	xxx				
21	xxx	xxx	xxx		
24	xxx				
27	xxx				
28		xxx			
30	xxx				?
33	xxx				?
35		xxx			?
36	xxx				?
39	xxx				?
42	xxx	xxx	xxx	xxx	?
45	xxx				?
48	xxx				?
49		xxx			?
51	xxx				?
54	xxx				?
56		xxx			?
57	xxx				?
60	xxx				?
63	xxx	xxx	xxx		
66	xxx				
69	xxx				
70		xxx			
72	xxx				
75	xxx				
77		xxx			
78	xxx				
81	xxx				
84	xxx	xxx	xxx	xxx	

*Brackets show cyclic phases combining.
†Note changing Pluto square Pluto.

none of the cycles work that way in reality. Minor cycles make a return every year or so, and our emphasis will be on maturation and individuation cycles, which take place as follows:

> Mars returns to its natal position every 2 to 2½ years
> Jupiter returns to its natal position every 12 years or so
> Saturn returns to its natal position every 28 years or so
> Uranus returns to its natal position in 84 years
> Neptune returns to its natal position every 164 years
> Pluto returns to its natal position every 248 years

In an average lifetime, we could experience about thirty-four Mars and seven Jupiter returns, three Saturn returns, maybe one Uranus return, and some change in the Neptune and Pluto cycle as these planets relate to the consciousness symbolized in the birth chart.

It is important to remember that the actual time span for each cycle will have to be plotted individually. Although you don't really need to know the birth time and place, you will need to know the birth year in order to do this, as the Pluto cycle is now moving very erratically. For example, someone born in the late 1920s will experience Pluto square Pluto around the age of 60, while someone born in the middle 1950s will experience this energy starting as early as age 33. Obviously the two individuals will experience the cycle very differently because of the disparity in the maturation level. (Pluto energy reminds me of the accelerated consciousness of this century.)

To go back to the planetary motion for another minute, if Saturn moved at the same rate of speed for everyone, we would all experience the Saturn return at age 29.46 years (or 10,760.27 days). Uranus should oppose itself at exactly age 42.01, so we could pinpoint midlife crisis. It doesn't work that way. Table 1 shows the average ages of planetary stress based on the cycles. Note how more than one cycle can be in effect at the same time, and also note the change in Pluto.

ASPECTS

In our discussion of cycles, the major emphasis will be on the hard aspects. We will work with the conjunction, square, and opposition as the planet moves in its orbit. To start the cycle, the planet appears in the natal chart and then begins to move (by transit). As it completes one revolution around the chart, it will return to the same place it was on the day you were born. This would be called the first return (such as the first Saturn return at age 28 or so). Figure 1 shows four phases of one cycle. It is interesting to note that these divisions of the cycle actually form a cross of life, and this is where both the pain and the energy are. The cross created by the constant cyclic movement of 8 planets and 2 luminaries creates a continuing shift in priorities, and could be visualized as a kind of kaleidoscope.

Some people will complain that I'm not spending a lot of time on trines and sextiles. I haven't because I don't want to. Suffice it to say that if you grow, the chances are it will be done on the hard aspects. When you study natal astrology, teachers usually mention that the most accomplished people have the most difficult charts. Hard aspects indicate sources of energy. So the crisis brought out by a square or an opposition, and the new beginning symbolized by the conjunction, can symbolize unfocused energies that we need to learn to harness so we can begin to benefit from our sextiles and trines.

Essentially, trine and sextile periods can be used to reap the benefits of the work done on the hard aspects. If we learn to focus energy constructively, the 60° and 120° periods will be comfortable. Trines and sextiles in the cycle can be plotted so the period can be

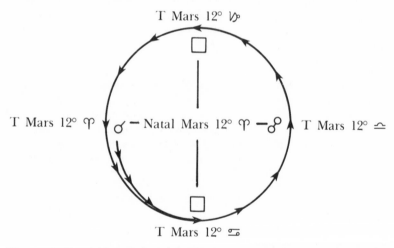

Figure 1. If natal Mars is at 12° Aries, the exact conjunction, first square, opposition, and last square will happen when transiting Mars is at 12° of the cardinal signs. The energy begins to manifest when transiting Mars passes 2° of the cardinal signs.

counseled and used to full advantage. Soft aspects seem to handle themselves; they don't require the counseling that hard aspects do. Most clients don't go to an astrologer to understand why they feel so happy—they go because they want to learn about something that makes them feel uncomfortable.

How to Calculate Periods of Stress

The cycles we are discussing are basically a particular kind of transit. Each planet moves from its natal place to the first square (Saturn square Saturn), then to the opposition (Saturn opposing Saturn), on to the last square (Saturn square Saturn), and back to the beginning (Saturn conjunct Saturn). This is very easy to calculate. All you have to do is look up Saturn's movement in an ephemeris and note when it comes close to an aspect to itself.

When looking backward or forward in time for a client, the average cyclic motion mentioned on page 5 will be of assistance while trying to determine what month or year to look for in the ephemeris. After working with the cyclic motion for a while, you'll know that every seven years or so Saturn will form another aspect to itself.

Orbs

Now we come to the uncomfortable issue of orbs. This is a hotly debated issue among astrologers, and I suggest that the orb should be determined after considering what you want to use it for. If someone is doing strongly event-oriented predictive readings, a small orb is in order. Likewise if you are working with midpoints, harmonics, or progressions. But when working with a transitory period, or with a cycle, a larger orb should be considered. Personal growth, stress, and cyclic activity have one thing in common: In order to change there must be a beginning, a gestation (or ingestion) period, and a result. If we use an event-oriented orb to predict growth, that implies that growth is not a conscious process but something that just happens to us. I frankly don't believe this to be true.

The farmer plants his seeds, raises a crop, and picks his harvest. If you plant carrots, you don't get potatoes from the carrot patch. If you plant stubbornness and immaturity or rigidity at the beginning of a Saturn cycle, you probably won't get maturation out of it—you will be more apt to get depression, anger, and frustration. So in order to counsel the growing process in yourself, or in clients, it is necessary to allow the time to be "pregnant" with a new focus of energy. We seldom like new energy and often don't handle it well. But if we can smell the smoke we might know there is a fire around; likewise with a large orb, we know the crisis is on its way. We get in on it from the beginning, have a chance to wrestle with the energy, and also have a chance to grow.

I use a ten-degree applying orb. If natal Mars is at 12° Aries, the energy begins to come into focus at 2° of Aries. The pressure will build until the aspect becomes exact, and when Mars passes off the 12° point, the pressure is over. For some reason the waning (or separating) aspects don't seem to mean very much, especially if you have worked with the applying aspect from the beginning. When Saturn is involved, the ten-degree orb means that you will be dealing with the Saturn process for about a year. During that year you will have a chance to see what you do that needs to change, and you can see what you are doing that causes your own limitations. You will also have the option to make some adjustments. If you don't learn quickly enough, the world will let you know. Something will happen that will cause you to become conscious, and we will discuss this in detail later on.

To digress for a moment about the orb issue: most astrologers say that astrology is not fatalistic, but the counseling they do is based on a small orb and a client winds up hearing event-oriented predictive material. Sometimes a need to predict or to amaze a client becomes an issue, and you hear, "watch out for November 11th." By counseling with a larger orb, you eliminate "daily predictions" by giving the client an option for taking charge of his or her own life. You are pointing out possibilities for change and letting the client decide whether or not to take part in the process of these changes, which is a completely different kind of predictive technique, and it could even be considered the therapy of the future. Many clients looked at me blankly when they were told they had a year of Saturn-type growth coming up. And they didn't much care for what they heard—"What do you mean a *year?*"—until the process became conscious and actually started to happen in their lives. They could relate to what was going on inside, and suddenly they knew they could do something about it. Instead of rebelling and becoming angry—or getting depressed—they were able to respond to the energy in a constructive manner, and often called to share their new understanding. The alternative is to let the growth process take place without being aware of it. This is the "victim of life" game, for you don't share in the birth of your new personality or your new cycle. Not much fun.

RETROGRADE MOTION

Planets move forward, stop, and then seem to move backward in the zodiac. This is an illusion, but the illusion of retrograde motion does reactivate aspects, bringing energy back to the planet in question. This means that a cyclic phase can be in effect for two or even three different periods of time, as you will see from some of the tables presented later in this section.

A number of students have asked how retrogrades work as far as interpretation goes. They seem to work this way: we get the first feeling of a particular phase in a cycle (say natal Saturn is at 2° Aries and transiting Saturn has moved up to 27° Pisces) and begin to realize that it's happening. Maybe we get uncomfortable, and in the case of a Saturn transit, a bit depressed, dour, and reality comes crashing in on some idea we had and it hurts. Saturn goes retrograde, the energy is released, and our universe lightens up when Saturn gets away from the ten-degree orb. Then Saturn comes back to 22° Pisces again, moving in on 2° Aries, and when it comes back, it seems to be moving faster. By this time we have had some experience with the energy; we know when it comes back because we can feel it. We work through whatever the aspect means to us until it passes by 2° Aries, and it moves on only to stop. It retrogrades back over the 2° Aries point and goes back into the late degrees of Pisces and stays there for a while. If we have worked with the symbolism of the cycle, this should be a time for cleaning up something that needs to be cleaned up. We don't have to worry about what "it" is, because if we pay some attention to our lives, we'll know what it is. Not something difficult to find—not something to be afraid of—just something to acknowledge. The cleaning up feels good; we may even volunteer for it. If we haven't done all we could, however, this may be a period where we are really put to the test, and we do have to get our act together.

COUNSELING CYCLES

We are going to discuss counseling in Part 3, but I do want to mention something about it here, close to the section on orbs and retrograde motion. I feel that cyclic phases, and especially hard aspects in cyclic phases, symbolize energy that pushes us to grow. The hard aspects signal that we are out of balance in relationship to the role that our stage of life demands. We need to regain or restore that balance, and this needs to be counseled.

On the one hand, each cycle has a life of its own; on the other, it relates to other planetary configurations within the natal chart. For example, any phase of the Saturn cycle will be affected by the natal aspects to Saturn, and these natal aspects will alter the growth experienced by the individual. Both situations will be experienced: the Saturn phase is available, and the Saturn phase will also alter that person's reaction to natal Saturn aspects, and how the natal aspect colors the various life activities that apply to the changes taking place.

In order to counsel the cycle we should keep in mind that the client must experience the next phase of life, the astrologer needn't protect the client from his or her own maturation. Neither should we counsel from a fearful point of view. In Part 2, I've mentioned some unpleasant events that may take place as a part of a particular cycle. This doesn't mean that this cycle will be unpleasant for everyone who experiences it, but that some people, with the appropriate natal chart and environmental conditioning, may not have an easy time of it. Sometimes we are able to communicate in an extraordinarily personal way with a client, and the communication helps someone avoid a trauma. Sometimes we can't. Each astrologer is stuck with the personal responsibility of determining how to communicate to a client, and how much to communicate.

Several students have asked me what the difference between good and bad really is. I don't know. A good experience for one person may be a devastating experience for another. Learning to balance the energy between "good" and "evil" energies requires that we understand the balance inherent in both sides of any polarity. Some people have found an exploration of William Gray's qabalistic work entitled *The Tree of Evil*[2] an interesting dissertation, as it is a discussion of learning how to balance polarities. Blind goody-two-shoes counseling that is full of love and gop doesn't help a real problem, and neither does strongly fear-oriented counseling. We must find the balance in between, so we can share this balance with our clients.

---

[2]William G. Gray, *The Tree of Evil*, Samuel Weiser, Inc., York Beach, ME 03910, revised edition 1984. A good discussion of the balance of energy and the polarity of good and evil.

MINOR CYCLES

The Sun, Mercury, Venus, and the Moon comprise the minor cycles. In terms of the growth process, taking all the planets into consideration, I don't feel that these minor cycles are terribly significant. Philosophically it seems far more important to reach out to Saturn or the outer planets in order to determine long-range life plans.

The minor cycles move very quickly; Table 2 shows the Sun, Mercury, and Venus returns for a ten-year period, just to provide something visible to relate to the cycle theory. The Moon returns to its natal position every 28 days, so we experience a lunar return once a month. When too much energy is concentrated on these minor cycles, it seems that the long-range plans of the larger cycles might be overlooked, causing the individual to miss the mountaintop because of the cracks in the sidewalk.

Minor cycles have been included here because they indicate certain kinds of energy and activity, and can be used constructively. My point is that this is not the most important place to start. I would recommend working most closely with the next section for Mars, Jupiter, and Saturn cycles represent the maturation process.

Table 2. The Sun, Mercury, and Venus return dates 1928-1938*

Sun 18° ♑	Mercury 18° ♑	Venus 6° ♐
Jan. 9, 1928	Jan. 9, 1928	Jan. 9, 1928
Jan. 9, 1929	Jan. 1, 1929	Oct. 28, 1928
Jan. 9, 1930	Dec. 25, 1929	Dec. 12, 1929
Jan. 10, 1931	Dec. 20, 1930	Oct. 25, 1930
Jan. 10, 1932	Jan. 28, 1932	Nov. 13, 1931
Jan. 9, 1933	Jan. 20, 1933	Dec. 26, 1932
Jan. 9, 1934	Jan. 13, 1934	Oct. 17, 1933
Jan. 10, 1935	Jan. 6, 1935	Nov. 27, 1934
Jan. 10, 1936	Dec. 30, 1935	Jan. 9, 1936
Jan. 9, 1937	Dec. 22, 1936	Oct. 28, 1936
Jan. 9, 1938	Jan. 31, 1938	Dec. 12, 1937

*Planets taken for Jan. 9, 1928 birth data using a midnight ephemeris.

Sun Cycles (365¼ days)[3]

The Sun symbolizes the "I am" part of the self in the natal chart. It represents the life force in the body. The transiting Sun seems to move through the zodiac once a year, and the *solar return*[4] indicates the Sun has returned to the exact degree, minute, and second of the sign it was in on the day you were born. In the cyclic process, this is an energy flow.

Everyone knows that the life force is very delicate in the newborn babe. Thanks to modern medical developments, the occurrence of infant mortality is now insignificant. However, the birthday period could be said to spark off an unconscious energy low that relates to physical birth, and repeats itself every year. This loss of vitality may possibly account for the fact that certain people die around the birthday, especially when they are older and the death is natural (as contrasted to death caused by serious illness).

Knowing how to use the Sun cycle can be beneficial to those who consciously work with the energy. First of all, we now know that there are four basic energy lows that will occur during the year. These energy lows are not caused by some unknown kind of depression—nor are they caused by the fact that we have done something wrong. The birthday period becomes significant because it indicates a time when we need to slow down. In order to avoid the cold or flu that we get when we push our endurance to the limit, we know that the week before and after a birthday is the period when we need more rest than usual. Perhaps we should diligently take our vitamins. Maybe we can lighten up the work load so that we don't push unnecessarily.

It has been said that the pagans began to celebrate birthdays to encourage loved ones to keep the spirit of life alive. Presents were given and parties were made for the birthday people to cheer them up. If the pagans celebrated birthdays for a reason, maybe we can as well? Allowing a bit of a party, and letting our friends know it's our birthday will spark a few birthday cards and maybe even a few gifts. For those of you who hate birthdays, has it ever occurred to you to find out why? Maybe the idea of getting presents and being shown

---

[3]Actually, according to Dal Lee's *Dictionary of Astrology*, it is the earth that moves around the Sun in 365-¼ days. But for our purposes in astrological symbolism, we look to see when the Sun returns to its natal place.

[4]The solar cycle of the Sun is not to be confused with the solar return that is calculated by some astrologers and used as a predictive tool.

love and affection is not a comfortable feeling. Maybe you think you don't deserve it. It could be you don't realize that the self-evaluation process you go through during your birthday is very much tied in with legitimate New Year's resolutions.

We spend a lot of time making empty promises that we don't keep when we get together to celebrate the old year out and the new one in. The people who keep the New Year's resolutions made on December 31st are usually the folks born on that day. The rest of us celebrate the old year out the night before our birthday, and the new year comes in when the Sun returns to the place it was when we were born. This is the time to consider the last year's accomplishments and to restructure our direction.

People who avoid birthdays may not like the depression that is felt at that time. "Oh, I don't want a birthday party, I don't feel good when it's my birthday, I hate this time of year, I just want to forget that day." Well, that may be someone's way of not coping with the depression that joins us for the blessed event. Because of the layman's interest in psychology, and because so many people have misinterpreted what they've read, most people equate depression with something bad or unhealthy.

Depression is a very healthy state when it is used properly.[5] During a depression we reach inside to ponder upon certain issues that need to be handled from within. These issues are usually private and are not easily discussed with others. The inner self is so preoccupied with the thought process that very little energy is left for outer-directed activities. Thus, what is called a depression develops. We astrologers can use the birthday depression from a healthy standpoint. And we can encourage our clients to understand it too.

How? Evaluate consciously what you want to do for the coming year. Remember what you decided to strive for last year. Whether you know it or not, your inner self is comparing last year to this year. How did you measure up? Most people are extremely hard on themselves, believing that last year's accomplishments—whether the plan was to mature emotionally, or develop at the career level, or whatever—were not good enough. When the depression occurs, most people don't have a realistic picture of exactly what was learned over the year. When actual accomplishments are considered

---

[5]The depression caused by an *internal process* is not the same as the depression defined in psychiatric terms. Chronic depression should not be confused with what I'm talking about here.

from one birthday to the next in a clear and precise way, it's amazing to see how much many of us have grown! And it's amazing how good we feel when we can consciously recognize our growth.

There are three other low vitality periods during the year. They are easily calculated, for they occur when the Sun squares itself, opposes itself, and squares itself again. Some people find that the first square is more difficult than the second, or vice versa. In order to get ready for the minor lows, pencil the dates in on your calendar ahead of time so heavy work commitments or strenuous vacation plans can be avoided during low vitality cycles.

If the new year's resolutions made on the birthday relate to the Sun cycle, it would stand to reason that these resolutions would be reassessed during the square and opposition periods. Perhaps the square will require that you adjust some theory that you have been holding; perhaps the "plan" needs to be altered to include something you just learned. It could indicate that depressions felt during a square or opposition period might be based on inner-self-work relating to birthday-time decisions. If we look into the cause of these periodic lows, depressions can lighten because they are more quickly understood.

When the Sun moves into a sextile or trine to itself, you will notice an energy high. This might be a time to keep in mind when scheduling a heavy work load or when planning a vacation that takes a lot of effort on your part. Not that you shouldn't take a vacation when the Sun is in hard aspect to itself—but better to take a beach vacation during that time. Save the mountain climbing in the Canadian Rockies for a high vitality period.

The energy highs symbolized by the trines and sextiles can be used to accomplish some of the goals we set for ourselves at the birthday resolution time. If we made a resolution to move forward on the job, it would make sense to talk to important people when the Sun trines itself. Making any kind of sensible move that relates to major goals can be handled better when our vitality is high and our outlook enthusiastic.

If we note that we have highs and lows during the year, we can begin to make adjustments to compensate for the energy flow. Are we down and depressed because we're tired? Are we feeling bitter because we haven't taken care of our health needs? These adjustments may tie into the Sun cycle energy, and if this is the case, we may help ourselves by tuning into our natural rhythms.

Mercury Cycles (approximately 365 days)[6]

Mercury in the natal chart signifies how an individual communicates. Communication manifests on many levels—it's not just how we talk. It indicates how we see, hear, or integrate the five senses into our knowledge of ourselves. The timing of the Mercury return will relate somewhat to that of the Sun, but we need to remember that Mercury goes retrograde from time to time, so the cycle will vary every year.

The Mercury cycle is not particularly important in terms of vast personal change, as most of us don't really think about "how we think." We may find ourselves adjusting the words we use, as well as our sensory perceptions, and these adjustments are based on our life experience. If the way we communicate doesn't get us what we want, we either complain that no one understands us, or we alter our behavior. Alterations made will be based on how old we are, for we seldom understand what it means to be hurt until we have felt some pain, and we don't understand how a wrong choice of words can affect our future until we have actually felt the result.

The Mercury return is not going to be important to a seven-year-old, as children are more involved in learning to express themselves in the universe. Energy is directed outward. As we grow older, and as we develop an interest in self-awareness, the timing of the cycle may be helpful. For example, if a diary is kept, and thoughts are recorded the week before and week after the Mercury return, we might see a pattern emerging in a few years. At times this cycle will take place at the same time the Sun returns to its own place, and watching the effect of the energy could be an interesting five-year study.

Venus Cycles (225 days)

Venus and Mercury are closely aligned with the Sun. The birthday low felt at the time of the solar return will be much more apparent than the Venus return. As with Mercury, the Venus cycle will vary every year, and Venus in the natal chart may be very close to the Sun or not, which will also affect the cycle.

---

[6]See Table 2, page 11.

In the natal chart, Venus symbolizes the "I want" nature. As we develop, the natural appreciations signified by the sign and house of the natal Venus placement will change. Or not. One would assume that with maturity would also come a heightened awareness of how to use the energy symbolized by the sign of natal Venus. We could also work toward making conscious adjustments in how we express the Venusian part of our nature.

It would be interesting to note what would happen if the Venus cycle were recorded every year. Perhaps we could more clearly see our developing personalities alter, and more readily understand what it was that caused the change. Looking at Table 2 on page 11, you see the staggered motion of the Venus return over a ten-year period. As far as plotting the cycles is concerned, I doubt that it would be worthwhile to do for children, but mothers may find it interesting. For an adult, a survey of the Venus return, as well as the squares and the opposition involved with the cycle, could prove to be beneficial if the personality is self-aware enough to recognize what happens.

Moon Cycles (28 days)

The Moon's cycle has not been included in Table 2 because the Moon returns to its own place every 28 days.[7] This means that we will experience a square, opposition, and another square each month. Using an applying 10° orb, that boils down to one rough day a week. We could be more easily upset or emotional on those days. The cycle can be plotted, but it won't be more interesting or informative than if we do the transits to the Moon on the same basis. In terms of long-lasting effects, this must be considered a minor cycle.

The Moon is not a minor symbol in the natal chart, however, and for our purposes in this book perhaps we should consider the comparison of the Moon's approximate 28-day cycle to Saturn's approximate 28-year cycle. The Moon has something to do with having a body, having an emotional response to life; it relates to

---

[7]The Moon's return is not a lunar return. A lunar return is used by some astrologers for predictive work. We are only discussing the transiting motion of the Moon here; the lunar return involves calculations that are not discussed in this volume.

feelings, the process of nurturing (not just being a perfect mother, but also the energy involved in making a garden grow, for example), and all that other good warm stuff. Saturn, on the other hand, represents authority, maturity, father and mother time, and the crystallizing of awareness. Perhaps we could say that the Moon responds emotionally without thinking about the results of the response at the moment, while Saturn balances out the energy by requiring that we learn how to become responsible for the emotional responses we have.

The Moon cycle does give us a chance to make an adjustment once a month. In the natal chart the Moon's key word is "I feel" and has a direct relationship with the "I am" principle symbolized by the Sun. Alan Leo said that the Sun represented the *Logos* and the Moon the *Soul*. The two combine to make a whole, and one cannot really be discussed without the other as far as the natal chart is concerned. The body renews itself every month, and the symbolism is especially clear for women, for the womb empties out once a month, and brings a new opportunity for life once a month. The physical renewal process would need to be compared with the Sun sign and placement to see how the Sun/Moon symbolism changed on a yearly basis. However, this is such a spiritually advanced theory that it would take a pretty well-integrated individual to be able to see it accurately; most of us are still preoccupied with assimilating more basic life struggles.

Phases of the Moon should be mentioned. We are not going into the subject, but the Moon cycle could be considered on several phase levels. The Moon has waxing and waning phases, and the new Moon (waxing) phase is more productive for some activities than is the waning phase. Farmers know that above-ground crops do better when planted on a waxing Moon, while root crops like the waning Moon phase. We know that we don't do elective surgery on a full Moon, as the chances for hemorrhage increase at that time.[8] In the personal sense, the phase of the Moon might be watched to see which phase is most comfortable to handle. These phases may be

---

[8]Many astrologers teach Moon cycles. I studied with Lynn Palmer, who not only taught horary astrology but has published several books related to using favorable phases of the Moon in daily life. C. C. Zain also wrote a pamphlet called *Horary Astrology: How to Select the Best Time,* available from the Church of Light in California. Selecting to work with certain Moon phases might be more commonly called electional astrology rather than horary, for horary implies the answering of a question, which is not what I'm talking about.

applied to planning and starting new enterprises, or they could be used for planning the best periods for your own personal activities.[9]

I would caution against the overuse of Moon cycles, for although they are interesting and can be used for other kinds of astrological study, to start with an overemphasis on Moon energy usually means you are ignoring the train wrecks in the rest of your cyclic experience. Please don't misread this and assume that I am saying the Moon is unimportant: In the natal chart the Moon's placement and aspects are *extremely* important to both men and women.

MATURATION CYCLES

These cycles are the key to the development of the individual. Mars in the natal chart symbolizes the action you take to represent your Sun and the Moon, and its activity involves your concept of action on all levels. In the old days Jupiter was referred to as the planet of expansion while Saturn symbolized limitation. That concept works if contemporary interpretation of what those words mean is adjusted to the subject being discussed. Expansion means reaching out if we are talking about personality, and limitation means holding in. The various phases of relating to others will tie into Jupiter symbolism, and various facets of rigidity, crystallization, and maturity would ultimately tie to Saturn.

These three planets are very exciting when they are considered in the light of the ongoing maturation process, as we can trace our growth and possibilities for change by observing the cycles. If we are lucky enough to work within the cyclic framework of these energies, our lives develop in an interesting way. If we get stuck in an old cycle, we don't develop to our full potential. The ancient philosophies made sense, and it is interesting to retranslate the meaning of cycles into a language that can be understood in today's context.

---

[9]Some people might want to work with lunar progressions, which is another way to look at changes in personality related to the symbolism of the Moon's movement. I would suggest Nancy Hastings, *Secondary Progressions: Time to Remember*, Samuel Weiser, Inc., York Beach, ME 03910, 1984; or Leyla Rael-Rudhyar, *The Lunation Process*, Aurora Press, New York, 1984.

MARS CYCLES (2-2½ YEARS)

The cyclic Mars energy is a very useful tool for personal develop-ment for Mars moves around the natal chart rather quickly—taking two to two-and-one-half-years to return to its natal place. In the natal chart, Mars symbolizes "I act," and it is through the Mars energy (its sign, house, and aspects) that the Sun has a chance to express itself. Mars transits to natal planets have been discussed elsewhere,[10] and here the emphasis will be on how to make the cycle work for you. Table 3 on page 20 shows a 10-year period of Mars action. Because the cycle is erratic, you need to plot it ahead of time. Each phase in the cycle lasts for about two weeks.

The Mars cycle is one of the most productive forms of energy available to anyone wishing to work with natal chart energy to change it. This cycle can be used to develop skills, enhance career, or improve relationships. It can be used to form the basis of future career moves or the beginning of a productive relationship. The sign natal Mars is in indicates what kind of energy is normal for you. A person with natal Mars in Aries will act differently from a person born with Mars in Capricorn.

The aspects to natal Mars will affect your ability to use the energy of the cycle. For example, if you have a natal Moon/Mars square, you will have to discipline this energy in order to tune into a new Mars cycle productively. The aspect signifies an individual who may act (Mars) against his own emotional nature (Moon), or may signify one who acts against his physical well-being (Moon symbolizing the physical body in this case). Depending on all the other factors in the natal chart, and depending on the age and environmental background of the individual concerned, the energy may need to be altered via conscious effort on the part of its owner. This individual may have a tendency to anger easily (not the best factor when considering asking the boss for a raise), or may be overly moody (a factor that might influence a promotion or the lack of one). The aspect may indicate the individual found the party last night more important than the interview he missed today. All in all, the Moon/Mars square may prevent him from taking advantage of the beginning of the new cycle. This behavior can be altered.

Or consider a person with a natal Mars/Saturn conjunction. The Saturn influence may inhibit Mars from taking action. The

---

[10]In *Transits: The Time of Your Life*, see my discussion on how to work with Mars transits to the natal planets. These transits shouldn't be confused with the Mars cycle.

Table 3. Mars cycles from 1980 to 1990*

Aspect	Date	Aspect	Date
☌	Oct. 31-Nov. 13, 1980	☐	Oct. 1-Oct. 17, 1985
☐	Feb. 24-Mar. 9, 1981	☌	Feb. 25-Mar. 15, 1986
☍	Jun. 24-Jul. 9, 1981	☐	Dec. 16-Dec. 30, 1986
☐	Nov. 13-Dec. 3, 1981	☍	Apr. 26-May 11, 1987
☌	Oct. 9-Oct. 23, 1982	☐	Sep. 13-Sep. 28, 1987
☐	Feb. 4-Feb. 17, 1983	☌	Jan. 28-Feb. 13, 1988
☍	Jun. 5-Jun. 20, 1983	☐	Jun. 13-Jun. 30, 1988
☐	Oct. 22-Nov. 7, 1983	☍	Apr. 2-Apr. 19, 1989
☌	Sep. 10-Sep. 26, 1984	☐	Aug. 25-Sep. 9, 1989
☐	Jan. 12-Jan. 25, 1985	☌	Jan. 6-Jan. 20, 1990
☍	May 16-May 31, 1985		

*Table of Mars cycles based on ♂ at 23° ♐ 30′. The conjunction varies from year to year, so this cycle needs to be plotted using an ephemeris. Also note that during the ten year period from 1980-1990, Mars is not retrograde in any of the mutable signs according to my ephemeris (*The American Ephemeris for the 20th Century*, Michelsen, A.C.S.).

Saturn influence may also cause feelings of insecurity or inadequacy, or even indicate a fear of approaching anyone in authority. In the latter case, the Mars cycle might find the employee grumbling to his friends about how no one on the job wants to do anything for him, and how he is basically unappreciated by his boss. We can't possibly know how a client will handle natal energy. Only by looking at the complete chart can we see the potential for the cycle. However, astrologers can be tremendously helpful to the client who wants to change his life, for we can point out the roadblocks that may keep the client from using the energy at his disposal.

I have encouraged certain clients to only use the Mars cycle for career for a couple of cycles when Mars was severely afflicted. The hard aspects to Mars in the natal chart were discussed and the client was aware of the kinds of behavior and reactions that might keep the Mars energy from manifesting on a constructive level. Anyone can sit back for two weeks and be careful about an energy pattern, especially when it becomes very important to a long-range life goal.

The energy works in the same basic pattern as all the planetary cycles. The new pattern of life is determined during the two-week period when Mars conjuncts its natal position.[11] When Mars moves on to square itself, an alteration in the initial decision must be made. Not that the original plan was inadequate—but during the first square, you learn something you need to know, and you need to alter your plan because it would work better with an adjustment. It is wise to remain flexible during this period rather than sticking to your guns at all costs, for this is a time when flexibility on your part will pay off.

When Mars moves to the opposition to itself, you will learn whether or not your plan was a good one back at the conjunction.[12] If it was, you will be reaping the rewards due you. If it wasn't such a good plan, you'll learn that too. We all make mistakes, and sometimes other transits and cycles are also taking place when the Mars cycle is operative. As we mature, we see things differently, and something that may have looked good a year and a half ago may not look so interesting today. We change. Mars is a part of that change, and a very helpful influence.

At the last square, something needs to be cleaned up. You may notice that something happens at work—some situation arises that you thought you put to rest a long time ago. It is the kind of event or situation that inspires a "Not *that* again!" response from you. This situation—the "not *that* again" situation—*must* be cleaned up and not swept under the carpet. For some reason, this particular aspect of your original Mars decision was not handled well, or it wasn't handled with enough maturity, or you were evading something, for whatever reason. The point is, on the last square we clean house. Face the music. Let the mess go. Own up if that's what the situation needs. But make sure that you clean up your act so that you don't take the last square with you into the next conjunction.

Mars cycles happen all your life long. During childhood this conjunction will mean very little for we unconsciously move into

---

[11]If your natal Mars is at 15° Cancer, the Mars cycle would begin when transiting Mars arrives at 5° Cancer and will last until Mars passes over the 15° point. When Mars reaches the exact conjunction, the cycle has been set in motion, and the effect of the cycle will last in some form until the next cycle begins.

[12]John Townley, in *Astrological Cycles* (published by Samuel Weiser, Inc., York Beach, ME 03910, 1977), said that the opposition signals a low period. Lionel Day said (in a lecture given in 1971) that the opposition indicates a time to reap benefits from decisions made at the beginning of the cycle. Townley uses statistics, and his "low" period probably indicates the expenditure of energy, as the focus of energy expended would be at the maximum at the conjunction. I don't think that these two people disagree, but they use different terminology to express the same idea.

our next Mars cycle. As we enter our teen years, some progressive young people may begin to use this cycle, but I really think this kind of information is better used by people over twenty-one. The older we are, the more life experience we've accrued, the easier it is to work with the cycle. One way to determine its usability is to go backward in your life—looking to see what you did over previous Mars conjunctions so you can see how the pattern works in your own life.

If you didn't know about Mars cycles before you started your last cycle, you may not be able to use the energy this time around. Some of us can remember what we were thinking about in regard to either relationships or career, but most of us can't, for the cycle only incorporates a two-week period. If you can't, you may have some glimmerings of the past when Mars moves to a square or opposition. If you can, you may say to yourself, "Oh God! Whatever was I thinking of!" At any rate, whatever has been put in motion can be lived through for it is not a dangerous cycle. It just indicates some time being wasted. Some clients bemoan the fact that a Mars cycle was missed, but this cycle happens frequently and is easily harnessed.

If you are interested in counseling people, you will find that you will learn a lot from observing other people's Mars cycles. Each astrologer draws a particular kind of client, and often there is a similarity between these people. Observing your clients' similarities will help you be more effective with the group you draw to you.

Also keep in mind how the Mars cycle ties into the present Saturn cycle, or Saturn transits in general. Decisions made on new Mars cycles are often changed drastically when a client experiences a major Saturn cycle or transit. This is too complicated to go into here, but the concept is something to keep in mind when watching the Mars cycle and the decisions that are made on it.

Mars and Career Development

In spite of yourself, when Mars moves to conjunct itself, you'll find yourself thinking about career. It doesn't matter what you do for a living, it matters that something about what you do needs to change because you are unhappy with the old system.

If you want to move ahead in your company, it's a good idea to plot the Mars cycle ahead of time. During the new cycle, you need to listen to your company's management people as well as to yourself. You may be promoted at this time. Without asking. You may be inspired to check out your future with the company. You may already know that the company will not move you into a better position, so the Mars conjunction would be the time to be out looking for a new job that offers the career advancement you want.

It is not unusual to do absolutely *nothing* during this cycle. Your friends may not see you doing anything visible in regard to a career change. You may be doing an awful lot of planning in your head, however, and it's very important to keep track of your thoughts. Write them down if possible.

How can you do nothing and still use your Mars cycle? Well, it's really doing something that no one else can see. For example, when I was getting ready to leave my nine-to-five job to become a full-time astrologer, I made my plans on a Mars conjunction. The plan included leaving the company, but not before I had paid off my car, set up an "insurance" fund in my bank account, and planned to have enough money to carry me through the changeover in career. One Mars cycle was "the plan" and the next Mars cycle brought the resignation. Slow and Saturnian, maybe—but one complete Mars cycle devoted to a total change in career. Clients have also told me that a Mars cycle seemed to be very low-keyed for them as they were gearing up for a major change. Not all Mars cycles are planning cycles, but some of them are.

A slow Mars cycle may occur when we are very young, and school isn't completed because a Neptune or Saturn transit is hitting natal Mercury. It could happen when someone is facing midlife crisis, and part of the crisis is a need to completely change careers. The Mars cycle can be quite difficult for the man who needs a complete career change in his early forties, for the additional pressure of family responsibilities may rest heavily on him if he doesn't have the needed support and encouragement from his family.

What if you don't have an exciting career to plan for? Maybe you are a young mother, or maybe you're a housewife with a comfortable routine that you basically don't want to change. Or maybe you have a job somewhere, and you make a living, but you don't have big eyes for a major career. The Mars cycle will still affect you. Life is like a game of chess, and the moves you make, the ideas you hold important when Mars conjuncts your natal Mars will have influence over your life for the next two years. The cycle will affect what you *do*, how you take action, how you view your life's work, no matter what it is. The squares and the opposition in any Mars cycle will affect you in the same way that the energy affects the most driven career person. The kinds of crises that occur, the obstacles in your path, the problems that must be handled may be different—but the pattern is very similar, and timing the sequence of events works the same way for you as it does for someone else.

Mars and Relationships

The new Mars cycle affects your love life as well as your career. Natal Mars symbolizes what you *do*—how you take action. Career is an issue, but so is sex. How are you going to handle your sexual relationship? How are you going to express your love? Venus symbolizes your appreciation of love, but Mars shows what you are going to do about it. Every time you begin a new Mars cycle your concept of love changes a bit. Many people end relationships on this cycle, and many begin one. Long-lasting relationships are renewed or brought to a different level now.

For the two-week period when Mars conjuncts itself, you are beginning to form a new attitude. Yes, you may be thinking about the job, but you're also thinking about the relationship that you have or don't have. You may want to make some changes, and most people don't use this period as constructively as it could be used because they don't know what is happening to them.

We all know people who poo-poo astrology. It doesn't work, they say. Astrology is just a bunch of gibberish, and the only people who use it are those who need to "believe in something." Right? Well, listen to these skeptics when the Mars return hits. Immediately you will hear conversation about new career goals, or some related discussion. And much more fun than work, you will hear pointed remarks being made about the present relationship or lack of one. The words usually go, "I have to do something about [name of other person]. He [she] is not putting out what I want. I'm not satisfied in my marriage [or relationship]." Or, if no relationship is on the scene, you'll hear conversation about how a new relationship is needed, and a definite interest in dating will be apparent.

How does the energy manifest? It's simple. When the conjunction takes place, and it's wise to know about it beforehand, you'll find yourself re-evaluating the present relationship. It doesn't matter whether you are married, living with someone, or dating. You will find something to complain about. This is not negative complaining; it's just that some adjustments are needed so you can better express yourself and become more goal-oriented. Most people don't handle this well. They say, "If *somebody* doesn't get their act together," or "If things don't change around here, I'm going to..." and you know the individual making this kind of comment is dissatisfied. Some people leave a relationship at this time.

When relationships end on a regular basis, it would be interesting to learn whether or not they all end around the beginning of a Mars cycle. Sometimes a pattern can be found, and counselors can help a client understand that a pattern lives in his or her universe, and this pattern is controlling the client's life— something that doesn't have to be. Just because a relationship needs adjustment doesn't mean it has to end. Obviously we don't all do this, but some people do, and when the situation can be counseled by simply understanding a Mars cycle, it's worth it. (You may also note that the Mars cycle ties into a natal Moon/Saturn aspect, or you may discover that you draw clients who have a particular aspect that ties into the Mars cycle, and this will enhance the lack of follow-through in the relationship department.)

To use Mars energy constructively in a relationship, bear in mind that you aren't the only person who has a Mars! You have one and so does your partner. You will dish out Mars behavior on your Mars return, and your partner will do it later. Since the cycle happens whether we know about it or not, it would be practical to join it instead of ignoring it. Rather than making empty remarks like, "If *some* people..." why not listen to what you are saying? What is wrong? Can it be discussed with your partner? Calm and sensible discussion will probably be well received by your partner, provided you don't start with accusations of inadequacy on the partner's part. Instead of being bitter, you can both work through whatever needs handling, and the relationship can grow deeper and more meaningful. Try to be open and responsive when you hear your partner's Mars cycle talking, too.

The alternative to working with the cycle is to let it use you. You may become bitter and sarcastic. Your partner may become bitter when the cycle hits in that direction. You both begin to pull apart—and where there were once warm and loving feelings, there remains only a bitter "marriage of convenience." Staying together for the children is not the best kind of relationship to have, especially if we are claiming any interest in becoming a self-aware and well-integrated person.

What is the worst thing that can happen if you talk to your partner? You can be rejected, that's what. Let's explore the concept of rejection for a moment. First of all, if you haven't had a good relationship with your mate for quite some time, why should this person be open to you now? If you are beginning to try to communicate after many years of not doing so, your mate will naturally be a bit suspicious. And if you resent your partner's suspicion, then frankly you aren't being very mature about the situation.

The other possibility in this rejection syndrome is that you may discover that you don't have a relationship. If someone loves you, that person will also listen to you. If someone loves you, that person cannot put down your ideas, your feelings, or what is important to you. If this is happening when you try to talk about your feelings to this person who claims to love you, then it's time to re-evaluate what your definition of love is, and what kind of a definition of love you want to live with. Some of us want the semblance of a relationship so badly we allow ourselves to be kicked, beaten, and abused—both emotionally and physically—just to have a body on our arm (or in our bed). That's okay if that's what you want, but if that's what you want, admit it and live with it. The other side of the coin is that on a Mars cycle you may end an unhealthy relationship.

The conjunction (a two-week period) brings up adjustments in your own mind as to what you are looking for, and what you need in your life to make yourself more comfortable. Usually sarcastic comments about a situation only cover up the real issue, which means something is going on that is making you feel unhappy, uncomfortable, or unfulfilled. The negative response only makes you aware that something is going on inside, and the negativity can be used constructively by getting to the core of the issue. If you make a healthy decision on the conjunction—you and your mate have a wonderful and warm discussion of what your romantic goals are, where the relationship is going—the next period for change will occur when you experience the transiting Mars square natal Mars. This is the first test of the cycle. Something needs to be altered. I don't know what that something will be, but whatever it is, the alteration will relate to the initial decision made at the conjunction. Something changes, and you work with it.

At the opposition the cycle is halfway done, and you will know if the decision you made on the conjunction was a good one. This will be a period of self-fulfillment. Some people have said, "You know, the new cycle brought up some unpleasant things in my relationship, but we tried to work it out. Now I can see that the work is paying off, for things are much better between us, and learning to talk things out has made our relationship much better." And sometimes it doesn't work that way because the partner is uncooperative. Maybe what you are looking for is unrealistic, or maybe it's not what you really want. You know the old saying that we want what we want till we get it. Sometimes we mature a great deal within the framework of a Mars cycle because other cycles and transits are happening at the same time. This change can't really be tied to just Mars energy, and at the opposition we discover we have outgrown the ideas we held just one year ago. When this happens, the opposition is the culminating point, and we ride through the rest of the cycle knowing that the new conjunciton will bring about a change from within.

At the last square, as in the career cycle, something needs to be cleaned up. For a two-week period we cope with an old emotional situation again, an old situation that has not been handled well the first time around. This is not something that you want to ignore, for it needs to be handled so you can get rid of it. Situations that are not cleaned up now will bring the dregs of some form of unpleasantness along with you into the next cycle. This square is not one to worry about. Some clients get really worried that they won't recognize what needs to be cleaned up. If you have any insight at all, you'll know. The situation is *old*, it is something that you already *know*. In my experience with students, clients, and friends, it has always been really obvious.

For example, a client of mine had an unpleasant experience with the Mars cycle, and she shared it with me. At the conjunction she discussed the possibility of marriage with a man she had been seeing for quite some time. She was in her late thirties, the relationship was rather permanent, they were seen as a "couple," and they were sleeping together. At this time, it was really important to her that they discuss where the relationship was going, for she did not want to play the role of mistress forever. She was ready to let go of the relationship, for she knew that he could reject her at this point. But he agreed: they should get married, they should make plans to make the relationship legal. Everything was fine.

At the first square, she learned inadvertently that he was dating someone else. That, too, was discussed! And at the opposition she broke up with him. Since they had discussed marriage he had become quite childish—not showing up on time, standing her up, not calling, generally not being a grown up—and this behavior hurt her a great deal. She was miserable for she really thought she loved this guy and didn't know what had happened.

On the last square he came back. He wanted to get back together he said. He had learned that she really mattered to him. He wanted to get married the following year and they even set a date. She was ecstatic. Then he borrowed some money from her. A lot of money. And she never saw him again.

The point I'm trying to make here is that you don't *start* something new on the last square of Mars to itself, especially when it's with someone "old." The clue is very clear. If an old relationship comes back within the two-week period while the last square is in orb, you are looking at some kind of problem. If you know your Mars cycle, when that phone call comes out of the blue you'll be able to enjoy the chat, but you'll also know that the call is not for you.

If you want to explore the concept of the last square, do it cautiously. The aspect is not dangerous, but I wouldn't loan money to an old lover on it. It might not be a good idea to move in with someone if you are going to give up your apartment to do it, unless you have a great deal of money. This aspect may put you in touch with some unhappiness, but it won't really hurt you or cause damage that would take years to repair. An unpleasant experience on the last square to Mars may teach you something that you will remember for a long time, so maybe the experience gained from experimenting with the cycle is worth it.

If you aren't dating anyone at the moment, it might be a nice idea to make yourself available to the universe when you start a new Mars cycle, as you might meet someone nice during this period. Granted you will also be interested in career moves, but not all Mars cycles are intense career ones. Be sure to listen to what you are saying to yourself in the social department. Please don't say stuff like, "I could date anyone—it's been so long since I've been out, I don't care who it is." Because down the cycle a bit you may care very much about what you said. Keep your energy constructive. Make sure your goals are high enough so you will be happy with them later on.

Natal aspects to Mars may cause some difficultly when you first start to work with the cycle. If you know that you have a Mars/Venus square, a Mars/Uranus opposition, or a Mars/Moon aspect, you will have to learn to handle your Mars cycle knowing that this energy is also active.[13] You may spend several Mars cycles "walking on eggs" until you understand how to use the energy to your benefit, but it can be done. By working with this energy, you will get to better understand yourself, and you can improve the quality of your life. When doesn't it work? When you don't really want to look at what you are doing. It's not the world doing it to you, it's you responding to the world.[14] During a new Mars cycle, you're the one who has to do the work. When you make the adjustments, or at least understand what you are doing to yourself,

---

[13]I don't want to discuss natal aspects here because they don't really fit in with our discussion of cycles. Natal aspects can be found in *Astrological Insights into Personality*, ACS, San Diego, CA, 1980, if you want to read my views, and there are many other fine textbooks available.

[14]I am not implying that one never gets mistreated in this world. Here we are talking about how to get your Mars cycle to function for you, and only you can do it.

you will have grown a lot. This may not be done the first time around, for this kind of inner awareness usually comes in retrospect.

JUPITER CYCLES (12 YEARS)

The Jupiter cycle repeats itself every 11.86 years, but let's use the figure of 12 years to make it easy on ourselves. In the natal chart, Jupiter's key word is "I relate." Dal Lee used the term *expansion* for Jupiter, and many astrologers see Jupiter as an expansive, outgoing planet, one that signifies good luck and abundance. These terms are nice, but in person-centered astrology the concept of expansiveness might better be called the ability to relate. Relating *does* have something to do with expansion, but Jupiter is not always a very expansive planet, especially when you really look at its natal aspects and the sign it's in! However you wish to define Jupiter for yourself, the planet has a cycle that occurs about every 12 years and important phases in the cycle will last about 2 months.

When comparing Jupiter to Saturn—expansion, restriction; relating and closing off; being idealistic or practical; philosophical or crystal clear—one can begin to see the interrelationship that the ancients assigned these planets. In the old days, seven planets were used and Jupiter/Saturn were the two generation planets that were tied to the concept of attaining consciousness. We'll discuss Saturn in the next section, but before talking about Jupiter it seemed important to mention these two planets together. Note seven planets, seven Jupiter cycles, seven years between each aspect in the Saturn cycle.

Jupiter returns to its natal place when we are about 12 years old. It returns again at 24, 36, 48, 60, 72, 84—all critical years in terms of life crisis. Table 4 on pages 30-32 shows the major crisis years in the various Jupiter cycles. Note the column indicating the average age for the Jupiter cycle as well as how this cycle will vary when you use actual data. Three different birth charts have been used in this table—one from 1928, one from 1941, and one from 1955—to show how the Jupiter cycle can vary. Again, this is a cycle that will need to be plotted using an ephemeris.

The Jupiter cycles symbolize certain normal relating changes that take place in the process of an entire lifetime. If we understand the basic cycle, the change from one phase of life to the next will not be so traumatic. It is interesting to note the pattern when you consider Jupiter the key to changes in relating.

Table 4. Jupiter Cycles and Crisis Years*

Aspect	Average Age	♃ 27° ♓	Actual Age	♃ 18° 8	Actual Age	♃ 27° ♎	Actual Age
☌	0	Birth	0	Birth	0	Birth	0
□	3	4/30/30-6/18/30	2	8/7/43-9/28/43 3/9/44-5/19/44	2-3	10/29/57-12/27/57 4/8/58-8/26/58	2-3
☍	6	11/3/32-3/19/33 7/2/33-8/31/33	4-5	11/2/46-12/24/46 6/17/47-8/14/47	5-6	1/14/61-3/4/61 9/4/61-10/14/61	5-6
□	9	1/29/36-7/1/36 9/21/36-11/23/36	8	1/8/50-2/23/50	8	7/1/63-9/18/63 2/14/64-4/3/64	8
☌	12	3/15/39-5/1/39	11	6/3/52-8/5/52 10/15/52-3/19/53	11	7/22/66-9/15/66 2/1/67-5/9/67	11
□	15	8/18/41-12/4/41 4/8/42-6/1/42	13-14	7/22/55-9/9/55	14	10/13/69-12/5/69 5/18/70-7/30/70	14-15
☍	18	10/15/44-8/15/45	16-17	10/18/58-12/6/58	17	12/29/72-2/14/73	17
□	21	1/10/48-3/21/48 5/11/48-11/5/48	20	12/20/61-2/5/62	20	6/3/75-11/2/75 1/17/76-3/17/76	20
☌	24	2/26/51-4/12/51	23	5/16/64-7/6/64 11/29/64-2/21/65	23	7/7/78-8/26/78	23
□	27	7/25/53-1/22/54 3/2/54-5/14/54	25-26	7/5/67-8/24/67	26	9/27/81-11/17/81	26

Table 4 (cont.) Jupiter Cycles and Crisis Years*

Aspect	Average Age	♃ 27° ♓	Actual Age	♃ 18° ♉	Actual Age	♃ 27° ♎	Actual Age
☍	30	9/28/56-11/26/56 3/10/57-7/26/57	28-29	10/1/70-11/20/70	29	12/13/84-1/28/85	29
□	33	12/25/59-2/17/60 6/26/60-10/13/60	31-32	4/8/73-7/24/73 11/30/73-1/21/74	32	5/14/87-7/17/87 9/22/87-2/27/88	32
☌	36	2/9/63-3/26/63	35	4/30/76-6/15/76	35	6/21/90-8/9/90	35
□	39	7/6/65-9/3/65 12/6/65-4/24/66	37-38	11/1/78-12/21/78 6/17/79-8/8/79	37-38	9/11/93-11/1/93	38
☍	42	9/12/68-11/4/68 4/18/69-6/28/69	40-41	1/16/82-4/5/82 9/13/82-11/5/82	40-41	4/15/96-5/25/96 11/25/96-1/13/97	40-41
□	45	12/9/71-1/27/72	43-44	3/16/85-9/9/85 10/27/85-1/4/86	43-44	4/26/99-6/16/99 11/8/99-2/1/00	43-44
☌	48	6/15/74-7/30/74 1/21/75-3/10/75	46-47	4/14/88-5/29/88	47	6/4/02-7/23/02	47
□	51	6/19/77-8/9/77 1/17/78-3/26/78	49-50	9/30/90-2/2/91 5/26/91-7/23/91	49-50	12/30/04-3/9/05 8/24/05-10/16/05	49-50
☍	54	8/27/80-10/17/80	52	12/22/93-5/14/94 8/20/94-10/20/94	52-53	3/10/08-7/12/08 11/3/08-12/27/08	52-53
□	57	11/23/83-1/10/84	55-56	2/26/97-4/26/97 7/25/97-12/15/97	55-56	4/9/11-5/26/11	55-56

Table 4 (cont.) Jupiter Cycles and Crisis Years*

Aspect	Average Age	♃ 27° ♓	Actual Age	♃ 18° ♉	Actual Age	♃ 27° ♋	Actual Age
☌	60	5/11/86-9/17/86 12/29/86-2/22/87	58-59	3/27/00-5/12/00	58-59	9/21/13-12/25/13 5/14/14-7/7/14	58-59
□	63	6/3/89-7/21/89	61	9/9/02-7/6/03	61-62	12/3/16-4/17/17 8/2/17-10/1/17	61-62
☍	66	8/11/92-10/1/92	64	12/3/05-10/3/06	64-65	2/17/20-12/10/20	64-65
□	69	11/6/95-12/25/95	67	2/9/09-3/31/09 9/10/09-11/15/09	67-68	3/24/23-5/8/23	67
☌	72	4/19/98-7/11/98 7/25/98-2/3/99	70-71	7/23/11-10/7/11 3/7/12-4/25/12	70-71	8/28/25-2/4/26 4/16/26-6/20/26	70-71
□	75	5/18/01-7/4/01	73	8/22/14-10/20/14 1/28/15-6/16/15	73-74	11/13/28-9/14/29	73-74
☍	78	11/30/03-2/8/04 7/24/04-9/15/04	75-76	11/17/17-1/14/18 5/4/18-9/13/18	76-77	1/31/32-3/27/32 7/14/32-11/18/32	76-77
□	81	2/22/07-5/19/07 10/19/07-12/10/07	79	1/24/21-3/11/21	79	3/6/36-4/21/35	79
☌	84	3/31/10-5/23/10 9/25/10-1/10/11	82-83	6/24/23-11/22/23 2/8/24-4/8/24	82-83	8/9/37-10/13/37 12/20/37-6/2/38	82-83

*Jupiter at 27°Pisces is from 1928, 18° Taurus is from 1941, 27° Cancer from 1955. Note that dates in this table include data from both the 20th and 21st centuries.

Cycle 1: Age 0-12: Physical expansion, learning to relate to the universe.

Cycle 2: Age 12-24: Sexual development, learning to cope with the development of sexual characteristics and the idea of becoming an adult.

Cycle 3: Age 24-36: Parent/child relationships, learning to become a parent, learning to relate at the level of parent/child.

Cycle 4: Age 36-48: Learning to teach others about becoming adults, sharing information, learning to give what you know.

Cycle 5: Age 48-60: Learning to accept help, letting go of children, allowing your children or others to help you if you need it.

Cycle 6: Age 60-72: Relating to spiritual development, seeing a different perspective in life.

Cycle 7: Age 72-84: Understanding the spiritual possibilities of life, learning to let go, learning to die.

To clarify what I mean by this, Jupiter symbolizes all forms of relating. On an outer-directed level, it symbolizes how we reach out to other people, what we expect from and give in a relationship—any relationship—including that of parent/child, child/parent, lover, employee, friend, neighbor, etc. All kinds of relating oneself to others can be seen by Jupiter's actual sign, place, and aspects. But Jupiter also signifies how and when we are pushed to move in the process of maturation. Different cycles in life require different things from us. A child is a child and not a parent, a parent is no longer a child, a person grows through many different phases of relating the self to the process of life.

Both Jupiter and Saturn cycles are very important to the process of individuation, and therefore I'm devoting a lot of space to them in this book.

First we'll discuss the Jupiter cycles one by one, for it is significant to watch how the various stages of life develop and how we are pushed to mature. Keep in mind that most people in this country are not told about the maturation process in life, and therefore are left high and dry every time they face a new phase of the life experience. We take normal transition periods to the therapist in order to get help in handling our crises, when in reality many of the problems we face are only related to growing up. If this is true, then the astrological counselor can be a valuable influence for clients who are undergoing the process of normal crises.

Jupiter Cycle 1 (0-12)

Here we are, a newborn babe, open to whatever the universe has to offer. We expect an awful lot from Mom and Dad, as we are completely helpless and unable to fend for ourselves. We receive whatever it is that comes our way—and our lives literally depend on it.

The first square to Jupiter occurs around age 3. The child has been born, fed, learned to crawl, walk, and is beginning to explore the universe. At 3 the kid is ready to hit the backyard. Alone. This is the first attempt at going out into the world on his own two legs. And this first going out is a very naive one—no concept of Saturn or danger—just reaching out and looking at new things. This is essentially when the child begins to open up to potential outside himself. This is the period when children begin to learn that toys have to be shared. Very often a new child is born into the family, or the kid is old enough to begin to be aware that time must be shared with other children. This is an age when kids turn blue a lot. Absolute rage. Sharing? Never!

At age 6 we come to the first Jupiter opposition, and we go to school. This involves a kind of separation from our parents, the beginning of reaching out into the universe as a person, which means we have to leave something behind. The ego must be subjected to the group need. Parents may feel a bit rejected. In the old days, a 6-year-old kid was old enough to help with the chores around the house or farm, and many 6-year-olds had jobs. Today we don't do that, but I wonder if it wouldn't be such a bad idea.

The last square hits at age 9 or so, and the child really begins to have relationships with other young people. In the process of trying to reach out to the world, the child will emulate the parent—and you will see the kid imitating the behavior of Mom or Dad, and being very grown up.

Jupiter Cycle 2 (12-24)

The second Jupiter cycle starts around the age of 12. The physical body begins to change. In the maturation process, the child has come full cycle as far as one phase of development is concerned. The next stage is the addition of sexual attributes in order to become a full-fledged adult. Many young girls start to menstruate; breasts and pubic hair appear. In the cultures where young men were circumcised, the 12-13-year-old boys were sent to join the ranks of the men in the tribe on this cycle. In some cultures the son was literally torn away from his mother to be part of a ceremony that joined him to the ranks of the men. We don't do this anymore, but the psyche of the young teenager still needs it. Consequently, the teenager feels a lot of pain going through a maturation process without any ritual support from the parent or society.

No matter how the family develops, and no matter how the child seems to be developing, the second Jupiter cycle means that this child is getting ready to reach out for the adult world, and the adult responsibilities of being a parent. The body is being equipped for it by developing the necessary equipment to produce babies and continue the species. The child's problems will mainly relate to how well he or she is prepared for this change. The body feels funny. Some youngsters don't develop as fast as their peers, and the proper growth rate for adult characteristics becomes very important. How the child will respond to this cycle will depend on the natal aspects to Jupiter. Parents should also note the difference between their respective Jupiter placements and that of the child. Obviously the child will not respond to teen years like the parent did if Jupiter is in a different sign or carrying a different emphasis.

The first square in the second cycle takes place at age 15 or so. The body is developing, the youngster wants to become more "grown-up." Young girls are biologically ready to reproduce, and generations ago many young women were married at this age and actually did start having families. Our problem in today's culture is that the 15-year-old female has the body of an adult and the mental development of a child. The psychic (instinctive or natural) drives of the individual are suppressed by our culture. Sometimes natural drives are suppressed by parents' values, which may not be adequately explained to the kid. We also tend to avoid discussing the realities of sex or sexual relationships with our children. So a dilemma arises.

For the young man, he's coping with a high squeaky voice and little control over his presentation. He may be gangly and awkward. He is beginning to relate to his sex drive but doesn't know how to handle it. He can't use it with social acceptance yet, but he is certainly looking for an outlet for the energy.

In some cultures where early marriage is not encouraged, young people find that the ages of 12 to 15 are strongly homosexual periods. The first reaching out for love or sex may be to someone of the same sex. When sex with the opposite sex is forbidden, natural sex drives may be repressed for varying reasons. Some children grow out of this phase and some don't. Parents should keep in mind that strong restrictions placed on the "goodness" of sex create complexes later.

At age 18, Jupiter opposes itself again, and we reach out to the world in a different way. At first we were reaching out to go to school, to develop friends. Now we are reaching out to leave the nest. We graduate from high school, leave home, go to college, get an apartment away from home, get married, have a first child. This is the time to leave home. We are now grown-up. This phase relates to the whole relating-reproductive cycle. The next place we take in society is that of "playing at being an adult." Why do I say playing? Because we are. We don't know it yet. The entire Jupiter cycle from age 12 to 24 is devoted to growing up. We may leave home at age 18, but we are still going to learn plenty more about being adults. In the first Jupiter cycle, the opposition meant that we pulled away from our parents to reach out for our peers. At the opposition in the second cycle, we leave home again, but now we are reaching out to relate to our peers as men and women. In the first cycle, our parents were hurt because they could feel us leaving the confines of home: parents were not the center of the universe anymore. At this second cycle opposition, we hurt parents again, for we reach out to develop our sexual lives.

No matter what our background is, this Jupiter opposition pushes us to move on. Each young adult will respond differently.

---

[15]Any discussion of homosexuality is bound to be misinterpreted by people who choose to for whatever reason. However, I thought it was important to bring up the possibility of teenage homosexuality, for it seems to be quite natural in some cultures. For example, in the Vigeland Sculpture Park in Oslo, Norway, young people are shown to be quite physically involved with each other at a certain age, and since this park was created to reflect every part of the ongoing life process, this must have been considered "normal" in the early part of this century in Norway at least. Young girls love each other, and young boys love each other. The first sexual experience and attraction has often been toward a friend. Sometimes this happens because it happens; sometimes it is engendered because parents placed too strong an emphasis on sex—teaching children that a normal sex drive is not "nice." Most young teenagers grow out of the homosexual stage, if that is what is meant for them. I feel it is important to point this out, for some parents are unduly worried about their teenage children, and some young adults think that because they have experienced a homosexual encounter, they are forever homosexual. That is not necessarily so. I also feel that strong urges for permanent homosexuality are indicated by the natal aspects in the chart, and homosexuality may be the choice of the individual who owns the chart regardless of parental influence.

Some marry, some leave home, some confront the world with great bravado, some are frightened by it. At one time, jobs were indicative of being able to leave home. Once a young man had a job, he could marry and continue on with his relating experience, although he probably didn't know what he was doing. A young woman often married to get away from home. Her relating experience was developed by being a young wife and mother. Today we don't live in such a narrow social structure, and young people need to find what it is they seek, knowing that parents cannot provide a ritual that will help them become initiated into this new stage of life.

Age 21 brings the last square in the second cycle, and this is when many young people come home after leaving at age 18. The decisions about relating to the universe didn't work out too well. For other young people, this time signals college graduation, leaving home, getting married if that has not been done already. At age 21 the young man is emancipated, being free to make loans, have credit cards, etc. Both men and women often marry at this time. It is an important stage.

For some young adults, the Jupiter last square is a very productive time, and for some it isn't. Celebrating the 21st birthday can be a major and enjoyable event. For some it's miserable. Problems at this age are usually tied to natal Jupiter aspects and can be understood when these aspects are considered. For the successful individuals, this is the beginning of life. The world is just opening up. For some, this cycle or this age is the most fun in life, for later cycles are not developed to their full potential.

Jupiter Cycle 3 (24-36)

The third cycle begins at age 24. The childhood phase is over; sexual development has taken place along with ensuing sexual experimentation and experimentation with adulthood. Now we enter the ideal young parent phase. The cycle functions differently for different people, depending on the level of development up until this point. For example, the biological urge to reproduce is quite intense at this time, and many young women have babies. If they don't have a baby, they want to. Some young women have abortions now; the inner drive pushes for conception, but a woman may choose a partner who isn't ready to marry, or she doesn't want to marry him for some reason. Pregnancy can also occur when a woman is almost through graduate school and the abortion is the result of poor timing for pregnancy. Poor timing? Not really! The biological urge is very strong now. Knowing that this energy is there can really help, for knowledge makes young women more careful.

Many young men marry at this time as the Jupiter return brings the parenting phase into play. When he is 24, she is usually 21. And a family is started. For those who don't marry on this cycle, the urge is often present. The parental phase manifests itself in some way. A nesting instinct is aroused, and single people become interested in making a home. Some avoid marriage, as the decision of whether or not to become a parent has not been settled. Some young women avoid marriage as the pregnancy question has not been faced for those who don't want children. This is not a pleasant concept to discuss in our culture, for all "nice" young women should want children. Certain aspects in the natal chart may indicate a reluctance to enter into the parent phase.

It should be kept in mind that it is not necessary to become a parent. It *is* necessary to consider the concept, because we cannot move forward making healthy adult decisions when we cannot look at our own motives. For example, the woman avoiding childbirth may date only married or basically unacceptable men. In this way, she can have a relationship that doesn't go anywhere; she can justify why she isn't getting married, and why she isn't having children, while claiming that all she wants is to find a good man and have a baby. She doesn't have to look at why she is doing this to herself. It catches up later, however.

Age 24 through 36 is the time when young adults reach out to establish themselves. The family, having children, and making a nest are very important to a farming society. Aggression, the conquest of new lands, and the enlarging of the king's territory are very important to the more migrant cultures. If someone is from a physical or spiritual heritage that relates to the herding group, we may notice that careers are built, and community status or travel is more important than nest building. People from a more agricultural background settle down and build homes. At any rate, the individual is trying to establish him/herself in the world, building a reputation as a responsible young adult. It is a reaching-out phase.

The first square in the third Jupiter cycle takes place three years later at age 27. This is the precursor to the Saturn return. We've gotten married, started a career, or haven't started a family, or whatever, and at the first square we begin to wonder if our decision at the Jupiter return was a good one. Relationship problems begin to enter the scene, and these are usually problems that are concerned with sexual relationships. Is my sex life satisfactory? Do I want to continue my sex life the way it is? Do I want to have more of a relationship? Many young people begin to complain about sex and marriage now, often because they are beginning to mature, which means they are beginning to require something. We tend to let our young people down for we don't provide much healthy practical training as to what to expect from a day-after-day marriage. Most young people think that love is romance, just like they saw it in the movies. But he has smelly socks and she looks terrible in the morning. Where did the romance go? And the children are squalling, the young couple have little time together and no privacy, etc., etc. Some changes need to be made about how the marriage and family relationship will develop, while still leaving room for the personalities of the people involved.

At the Jupiter opposition (age 30), the Saturn cycle has taken place and viewpoints are changing. Depending on how one survives the Saturn cycle, or how much has been learned from it, the Jupiter opposition functions accordingly. Young men have decided what to do with their careers. They got married at 24, at the Saturn return the grown-up goals were manifested (see next section for a description of the Saturn return), and at the Jupiter opposition they should be reaping the benefits of the decision they put into practice at age 24. In other words, they should have a well-started career, a happy young family, and they should be feeling good.

This may not be true. If the marriage was not planned well, the young couple may find that they have grown apart, that they have nothing in common but the children. The wife may not be able to keep up with her husband and his goals; and when he picked her, he probably wasn't thinking that he may need her to help host some of his business dinners. The differences in family background and environment may also come into play here. Someone in this relationship may not be happy.

For the young woman, she too has gone through the Saturn return, and is looking forward to her future, but she may not be happy with what she thinks her future is. If she didn't have that baby at age 24, she may want to have it now, and she can get pretty desperate about it. If she has children and is functioning under the pressure of the nuclear family structure with no relief in sight, she may become despondent. The nuclear family means Mom gets to take care of the kids seven days a week with no break, and usually her only companionship is that of other young mothers in the same boat. When this happens, we often see maternal burnout—the mother lives for her children, forgetting herself as a human being, forgetting herself as a companion to her husband—and you see her walking glazed-eyed around the supermarket, not even hearing the screaming and yelling of her children, a sound which would drive anyone else crazy. But we are forgetting the purpose of the Jupiter opposition. It's now time to look and see if the baby decision was okay. Do you have to give up your life to become a mother? Can you have children and still be a person? If the 30-year-old woman is to develop in any kind of an interesting way, she will have to think about these questions.

At the Jupiter opposition, single people are not facing the children dilemma. What they are looking at is the aging process. Thirty is a scary word to many single people; it was fashionable to be single in your twenties, but it's no longer such an interesting idea. What kind of a relationship are you looking for? Many people begin to develop different kinds of friendship now, as lovers seem to come and go, or they don't always work out, but a friend is around no matter what the weather. Changes in perspective take place.

At age 30 it's important to realize that life is not really all about being the 21-year-old Madison Avenue fashion image. Insecurity can be alleviated after you take the time to evaluate yourself. Physical beauty isn't all there is. If your husband is eyeing all the lovely young things in the office, either he can't handle a relationship, or you aren't giving him much to come home to. Becoming 30 means that we are not as dumb and naive as we were in our twenties; we don't fall for as much anymore. We have more to offer as we know more of what we like and don't like. For the male, becoming 30 means that he is being accepted as the young executive. He's no longer a child, he's proved himself out there in the world, and people are more open to accepting him than they were before. How he values the aging process is important, for if he thinks that youth can be maintained by buying a sportscar, then something may be missing on an inner-self level.

The last square of the third cycle hits at age 33. If the Jupiter return at age 24 wasn't what it should have been, the last square will bring that situation to life one more time. This is the time to clean up the cycle and prepare for the next one. Relationship problems need to be faced in some way. Some balance between loving children and having adult relationships may be the key here. Many single people I talked with said that this was a time to form new types of relationships. No longer could meaningless relationships be chalked up to experience. Friendships became more important. When a new love relationship was considered, it was from a very different point now, as it was more involved with conscious commitment.

The concept that we take with us at the beginning of a Jupiter cycle will stay with us for 12 years in some way. One client of mine lost her husband on that cycle. She vowed she would never love again. When she changed her mind, she couldn't find anyone to love, because when she found someone attractive, he wasn't ready to get involved. She could not break out of the effect of the cycle till the next one started. This may not happen often, but it may help some people understand how they can lock themselves into a thought framework that it takes years to work out of. A new Jupiter cycle is a relating concept that is being developed. For two months, the thoughts that go through your head are quite important, for they set the foundation for a twelve-year period.

Jupiter Cycle 4 (36-48)

This is a rough age for women and an easier one for men. Most men have been trained, via the social environment, to take on the pressure of the work world. The young man of 36 starts a new phase, that of relating to his work as a grown-up, a career man. He may think he will own the place by the time he's forty. He's no longer considered the bright young man with no experience. Work is power, and power makes you important, and the 36-year-old male is going for something in life. He wants to find a place for himself in the world, and at 36 he is still building. He hasn't realized that he's fallible yet, that he might not make it, or that he might grow old someday. He's smooth, if he is ever going to be smooth; he knows how to do things; he stands in the community in his own right. He may entertain ideas of playing around. You know, the wife is tired, busy with the kids, the PTA or the little league, and here is this beautiful young thing in the office....

The woman at 36 isn't functioning quite so well. If she has been trained to be a wife and mother, or if she traded femininity and personal development for an exclusive with her children, she may be feeling pretty insecure inside. This is the time when she begins to realize that the kids won't be there forever, and then what? No longer feeling attractive, and no longer sure of herself (how could she be after listening to ten years of kiddie babble?), she is looking outside herself for some kind of reassurance. If her husband is about the same age, he's off in his own world, and may not even see her. This means she may be very ripe for an affair. If she's basically a loyal type, she gets to deal with the guilt that ensues because she has a husband, children, and a lover.

A lot of women go into a body building phase, with the exercise class and the look-young program. But this exercise stuff doesn't do it when the real problem is an internal one. A great body is nice but it won't solve the issue of a lack of self-confidence. What do you really think you are worth? The kids are pulling away, and *who* are you?

Couples may divorce on this cycle or as a result of it. This is not the answer, for most divorces take place because people aren't communicating with each other. For both single and married people, this cycle means that the role we play needs to change once again. Goals need to be determined on some level, so that the relating side of life can be developed in perspective. The cycle will change many life issues, for personal relationships—lovers, partners, friends—will change, as will the role that you play in the community. The cycle doesn't portend phoneyness, but rather a change in the structure of relating. Parents need to pull away from their children. No longer does the kid need a bottle and a clean-up. The key here is instruction. At age 36, the parent could have a 12-year-old child, if a child was born when the parent was 24. So now is the time to teach the child how to survive. Now is also the time to start teaching and giving back some of what was taught to you, but this may create a certain kind of insecurity if you still don't know where you yourself are going.

Most Americans think there are two ways to be—young and old. In between is just a bunch of hazy years and better-forgotten memories that mostly concern the kid's graduating from 8th grade, etc. Not so. This is the time when men and women should be deciding what kind of person they are going to mature into. The business of raising kids is a part of it but not the whole of it.

We are supposed to become more self-confident as we age. When we were younger, personality and self were first and foremost. The parent stage broadens our outlook to include self and possessions, for when we are parents (actually during the 3rd Jupiter cycle), we reach out to accumulate. Often we accumulate "my husband, my wife"—a social position, "my son, my daughter"—another social position, "my house, my car"—more prestige. This is all a part of becoming the "best" adult and having the best and the most. The next phase is geared to teach us how to encourage other people to develop their potential. Helping others is actually the beginning of the development of the wise old man or woman syndrome.

The words matriarch and patriarch tend to scare many Americans, for we have a national image of the controlling mother and father, who won't let go of their adult children. A matriarch or patriarch can sink to the most petty level, and we do see the worst from time to time. But we don't have to sink, we can develop into constructive mature people, able to encourage others, using our experience and knowledge to help those we love grow. In our mobile and nuclear society, we don't contact family very much and may miss seeing how our older folk mature. In our past, however, we still hold a psychic memory of the heritage we come from, and that memory includes the roles played by older and respected members of the tribe. We will all take our place in the "tribe" someday, even if we haven't prepared adequately to play the role. Developing self-confidence about who we are can start to germinate now, especially if we know that our aging will incorporate the chance for wisdom.

So this next phase is a teaching one. We learn to encourage someone else to develop potential. This involves our kids, so mothers encourage daughters to become confident young women, and sons to become confident young men. Fathers do the same thing. People who can encourage others to function at their best, who are open enough to train others to take over a job, are beginning a different kind of sharing and relating. We may not like our new responsibility, but how can we develop into wise people if we are stuck in the mire of only expressing self? I'm not saying that we should not express ourselves, but that this Jupiter cycle indicates a need to develop another facet of ourselves. Perhaps the ability to truly share and nurture signals the development of unfeigned self-confidence.

Often part of the growth involved in the fourth Jupiter cycle involves a change in status. The kids are entering puberty, and your own parents are getting old. You end up being caretakers of two groups, your children and your parents, during this phase. Single people don't have the children, but many do have parents. Changing roles from being a child to becoming a caretaker of a parent creates quite a change in the psyche. Some people don't adjust to it easily. It's hard to let go of those early childhood memories when Mom and Dad were the center of the universe, and become the person who may be called upon to care for or advise these same once powerful figures. In a nutshell, this cycle is one where children are being let go emotionally, children are being taught how to become adults, parents take on a new phase, and we are teaching what we know to others.

At age 39, we see the first square in the 4th Jupiter cycle. If no major decision was made at age 36, or the decision was merely a bitter one made in response to the environment, or if you misunderstood the beginning of this cycle, this can be quite a crisis period. Forty is rapidly approaching. What did you do with your life? How much have you done that was important? How do you want to approach your forties? Some men become quite nervous because it doesn't look like they will own the company after all. Or they feel they are being left behind.

This is a difficult period for women as well. If the 36-year cycle was met with knowledge and a good Jupiter decision, the square will involve some alteration that is needed in the plan. If the cycle was ignored, whatever immaturity that needs to be handled will resurface. Forty brings on midlife crisis.

The Jupiter opposition hits at age 42. If the decision made at age 36 is working, you begin to reap the benefits and start to feel good about yourself. The work you did in order to establish this life phase is beginning to take effect. If the decision was immature or too self-centered, you will become aware of that. This would be the time to adjust your plan in order to make your older years more interesting. The opposition occurs around the same time that other cycles are in effect, so it can be an intense period for both men and women.

This Jupiter opposition may bring up the issue of health for you. Many people cope with illness in the family or with personal illness, for the high living related to Jupiter aspects may come home to roost. The body is beginning to break down, and if we overloaded our circuits, we may have to change our way of living. Remember the dinners you used to like when you were 27? How do they relate to the kind of food you can eat now? Health, and reaching out to others with sympathy and compassion may become an issue. A different kind of relating takes place for it ties in more with life and death.

The last square occurs about age 45 and the reproductive processes begin to fade away for women. Some react strongly to the idea of menopause, especially if the concept of self-worth is tied to the reproductive process. This is a time when many women go back to work, and if they start at this age, a feeling of inadequacy or a lack of self-confidence may be evident unless they took some time to go back to school between ages 36 and 45.

Men going through this square are coping with the leftovers from the beginning of the cycle. Some men discover that the decision made at age 36 was not one they would do again, and at 45 they eat a little crow in order to let the cycle pass. It is still a good time to clean up your act. The square is in effect for about two months, and this period can be used to clean up relationship problems, either at home or at work.

Jupiter Cycle 5 (age 48-60)

Age 48 starts the fifth Jupiter cycle, and we begin to consider old age. How are we going to grow older? What we decide to do now will be in effect till age 60, which is getting close to retirement. It's important to listen to what you are thinking during the two months that Jupiter sits on natal Jupiter because your inner self will start acting out what you are thinking. Pay attention. Write down your ideas. Listen to yourself.

At 48, the kids should be leaving home, so this is an important cycle in regard to marriage and personal partnerships. Whether you have children or not, you are now faced with a decision as to how to handle this aging process. Some will walk away from a marriage now. It just seems like a good time to end something that wasn't very pleasant. The marriage that ends at the beginning of this cycle is one that probably stayed together for the kids. The mother or father felt it was important for the children to have both parents, even though one parent was not particularly happy. Once the obligation of parenting is fulfilled (according to the drive within the individual), the unhappy partner leaves. Many husbands or wives are devastated for the partner is not leaving to run away with someone new. He or she is just leaving. It's hard to accept that you lived with someone who didn't like you for twenty years, and when responsibilities are fulfilled this person leaves you just to get away. Not nice. However, it happens.

If the marriage is to continue, the basis of the relationship has to change. This can be difficult as it requires that both partners expand the relationship. In what way? No longer are little Johnny's daily activities the talk of the household. No longer is dinner for the kids an important item. Well, what do you talk about? Some couples are delighted because they finally have a chance to be together again as lovers. They can make love on a Saturday afternoon for example. Many parents want the children to leave because they have given enough, and most children are not aware that Mom and Dad have a personal life.

The fifth cycle is uncomfortable if the marriage was not a communicative one, for two strangers now have to learn how to talk to each other again. It may make for a few tense moments! You don't have to be married to undergo these changes in the relationship syndrome. Whether you live with someone or not, whether you are hetero- or homosexual, the changes still take place. The subject matter varies; two gay men living together will not be arguing about what to do when the kids leave home, but something will be an issue and the people involved will have to face that issue.

Some of the tension of this cycle is caused by the fact that age fifty is a biggie to most Americans. It means ten or twelve more years to work. It means the aging process is happening and the senior citizen classification is getting real. Some people look forward to this and some don't. Personally I don't think we have a very healthy outlook regarding senior citizens. It's true that some older people just stop producing and become senile quickly, but everyone doesn't have to develop this way.

So far we've learned how to be an adult, we've learned how to give, and now we have to relate to the idea of taking. The youngster takes life as a matter of course, taking and taking until he or she builds something of value. The parenting stage taught us to consider someone else; then we had to learn to nurture or relate a different way—by teaching and bringing out potential rather than by just taking over. Now it's time to learn how to take again, so that we can move on in the process of being able to receive what we need. If we don't, there is a tendency to become rigid and stubborn, while trying to protect our autonomy. In order to be able to give the most back to our society, we need to ready outselves for the philosophical stage. We're not there yet, but we need to prepare. Accepting from others is a part of recognizing the stage we are about to enter. We will have words of wisdom someday soon and we open the door now by avoiding rigidity. This relates to becoming receptive. When you give to others, you stay in control; when you accept from others you can receive. Receptivity relates to spiritual development, for you need to become receptive to the voice within.

Retirement is another issue. It will happen soon, and what will you do? Some choose the retirement community, with people their own age and a nearby hospital. This is a personal decision, but once we move into a retirement community, we lose the vibrancy of youth and normal living. People who stay sharp often don't choose this way out. Some plan to leave business at normal retirement and begin to train themselves for a different occupation. That's a good idea. Work never killed anybody.

At age 51 we experience the first square. This two-month period will bring up more questions in regard to how to age gracefully, how to let go. Maybe some issues with the kids still need to be handled. Watch out for any feelings of resentment about accepting help or about feeling obligated to overhelp your kids.

Age 54 brings on the Jupiter opposition, pushing us again about this retirement business. If we are getting testy and scared on the job, we won't let anyone help us. Are you getting slow, or is the department getting bigger? Do you need help? Why not let the kids cook Thanksgiving dinner? Accept.

The last square appears about the age of 57, and any relationship problems that need fixing will return to the scene. Rather than avoiding the issue, it needs to be faced so you can move onto the next phase. Keep in mind that you are no longer a parent. You are a person, and your grown-up children are people too. You can't run their lives. You have to let them be what they are—adults.

Jupiter Cycle 6 (60-72)

This can be a frightening time, for retirement is looming close. The aging process is setting in for sure. Your bones ache and you can't do what you used to do. If your values are concentrated on lost youth, this can be an unhappy period. Actually women do better at this age than men, for women made their peace with themselves around age 50. Men are now confronted with this unpleasant business of leaving the office and staying at home. Hopefully some retirement interest or employment was arranged for previously so the transition from one type of work to another won't be too drastic.

This is the cycle that pushes spiritual development. Jupiter symbolizes relating, expansion, but it rules the sign of Sagittarius, which has always signaled the philosopher. So now the philosophical side of Jupiter is coming to the fore. In the Orient, at this age the householder leaves his home and possessions and goes off into the woods to find nirvana, or wisdom. We can do it too, but we don't have to leave our homes. This is a time to explore some kind of philosophical theory, metaphysics, or work with a church.

At 63 retirement has often taken place. Men may be already chafing at the bit because the Jupiter decision at age 60 wasn't a good one. If this is the case, this is the time for alterations on the original plan, as you now know more about what you want to do, or you may have suddenly realized what this cycle is all about. It's not about being lonely and forgotten. A whole new world has opened up. Some men get involved in helping others in a business sense, volunteering time as consultants. Some women get very involved in local organization work, although we wonder if it's done to get away from a retired husband who is staying at home too much.

The Jupiter opposition arrives around age 66, and this spurs on more activity in this aging process. If the plan at 60 was a good one, the benefits of the work done will start to show. This should be a very happy period for those of us who have retained our health.

Age 69 brings the last square, and with it all the pain of the bad decisions made earlier in the cycle. Anything that needs to be cleaned up should be taken care of. If some philosophical insight was missed, look at it now. If relationships with children and grandchildren are misunderstood, maybe you need to talk more openly with them. You are not just a grandparent but are also a person interested in developing something for yourself. Single people may need to solve another issue. Does it relate to acceptance?

Jupiter Cycle 7 (72-84)

The seventh Jupiter cycle involves the final stages of spiritual development. The whole point of considering the universe from a philsophical or spiritual viewpoint is to make our ultimate peace with life. When we are born, we first relate to our needs—food, roof, shelter from the unknown. As we mature, we relate to our changing bodies. We participate in the process of becoming parents and members of a social group. To what avail? Why is this thing called life happening? Where do we fit into it all? What has life meant to us? And what will death mean?

We are all going to die someday, everyone knows that. We will have watched many friends and loved ones die; how are we going to handle our own death? Exploring the possibilities of dying, connecting up with the local hospice to learn something about this very intimate process might be one phase of handling the issue. Death is the biggest thing that will happen to any of us since we were born. We know very little about the experience, and most people fear it, but a whole new kind of literature is on the market now for those who are curious.

Once dying is considered, living life can be fun, for the older person who has made peace with death isn't planning to die, but is able to live life more fully and with greater enjoyment. The winter of life has its own beauty.

The first square at age 75 may change plans made thus far. The decisions made at age 72 will be evaluated and there's another push for spiritual development.

At age 78 the opposition occurs, bringing more changes in regard to the idea of death being a friend or foe. This opposition is a final push for spiritual consciousness. This two-month period may bring great spiritual insight or understanding. Once that insight is obtained, more withdrawal from the family takes place and love can be given in a more universal context.

At age 81 we experience the final square, bringing with it the situations that need to be cleaned up and finished. We are getting ready to start the eighth Jupiter cycle, and we now need to face the issue of death.

Jupiter Cycle 8 (84-96)

This cycle starts around age 84. According to Lionel Day, 84 is the astrologer's end of life. Numerologically and symbolically this makes a great deal of sense, for we have lived through seven development cycles of Jupiter and three maturation cycles of Saturn. As the planets' orbs are changing, maybe this will change too. However, not everyone decides to die now. Many creative and happy people are enjoying life. An awareness of God and awareness of the universal consciousness are gifts that can be shared.

SATURN CYCLES (29.46 YEARS)

As we said in the last section, Saturn and Jupiter have a symbolic relationship. In the natural zodiac, Jupiter rules Sagittarius and Pisces, or the signs that symbolize philosophical and humanitarian development. In the natal chart, Jupiter symbolizes how and why you develop certain personal philosophical and humanitarian traits during the cycles of your life. Saturn rules Capricorn and Aquarius, signs that rule leadership, career, public image, the interplay between self and friends, as well as the realization of hopes and wishes. The public/private image, and the expression of self while interrelating with others can be understood by looking at the oppositions involved with the signs Saturn rules in the natural zodiac. The opposition between Cancer/Capricorn is also an opposition between the Moon and Saturn, or emotions and responsibility. The opposition between Leo and Aquarius is also an opposition between Sun and Saturn, or the expression of self and Aquarian responsibilities. Saturn is tied in everywhere the self goes to express energy or ideas in the natural zodiac, creating the symbolic image of responsibility for all activities involving Sun and Moon expression. This could be seen as restrictive, or it could be seen as the need to test the self in all its manifestations.

Table 5. Saturn Cycles and Crisis Years*

Aspect	Average Age	♄ 14° ♐	Actual Age	♄ 13° ♌	Actual Age	♄ 16° ♍R	Actual Age
☌	0	Birth	0	Birth	0	Birth	0
□	7	3/21/35-10/14/35 12/2/35-3/21/36	7-8	8/27/46-2/28/47 5/9/47-8/17/47	5-6	2/25/62-8/30/62 11/18/62-3/2/63 9/26/63-11/16/63	6-8
☍	14	6/9/42-5/30/43	14-15	11/17/53-6/15/54 7/28/54-11/21/54	12-13	6/23/69-10/22/69 3/14/70-6/11/70 12/11/70-2/24/71	14-15
□	21	10/28/48-2/6/49 7/18/49-10/17/49 3/21/50-7/8/50	20-22	1/30/62-2/4/63	21-22	7/26/76-7/17/77	21-22
☌	28	11/17/56-11/23/57	28-29	5/25/69-12/2/69 2/5/70-5/17/70	28-29	10/21/83-10/24/84	28-29
□	35	5/11/64-7/21/64 1/28/65-5/6/65 8/22/65-1/28/66	36-38	7/2/76-10/1/76 1/27/77-6/20/77	35-36	4/15/91-6/19/91 1/3/92-4/15/92 7/12/92-1/7/93	35-36
☍	42	7/27/71-11/13/71 4/13/72-7/10/72 1/6/73-3/24/73	43-45	1/3/83-3/26/83 9/25/83-1/1/84 4/22/84-9/27/84	42-43	4/22/99-8/15/99 9/14/99-4/13/00	43-44

Table 5 (cont.) Saturn Cycles and Crisis Years*

Aspect	Average Age	♄ 14° ♐	Actual Age	♄ 13° ♉	Actual Age	♄ 16° ♏R	Actual Age
□	49	8/28/78-8/23/79	50-51	3/7/91-8/2/91 12/4/91-3/11/92 8/23/92-12/6/92	50-51	9/3/05-2/20/06 5/19/06-8/24/06	50-51
☌	56	12/22/85-7/3/86 9/11/86-12/28/86 7/27/87-9/12/87	57-59	7/20/98-9/11/98 3/29/99-6/28/99 11/3/99-3/18/00	58-59	11/26/12-5/30/13 8/16/13-11/29/13 6/30/14-8/10/14	57-59
□	63	3/4/94-3/5/95	66-67	8/9/05-7/31/06	64-65	2/8/21-2/13/22	65-66
☍	70	5/23/01-5/13/02	73-74	10/31/12-11/4/13	71-72	6/1/28-11/23/28 2/17/29-5/24/29	73-74
□	77	10/7/07-3/10/08 6/26/08-9/28/08 5/7/09-5/27/09	79-81	1/13/21-1/19/22	80-81	7/10/35-10/10/35 1/22/36-6/28/36	80-81
☌	84	2/10/15-4/17/15 11/1/15-2/12/16 5/8/16-11/6/16	87-88	5/7/28-4/30/29	87-88	1/19/42-3/12/42 10/5/42-1/14/43 4/11/43-10/8/43	86-88

*Saturn at 14° Sagittarius is from the birth year 1928; at 13° Taurus, from 1941; and at 16°Scorpio R, from 1955. As you can see, the cycles sort of work, but at age 84 the cycle is way off. It may occur at age 84 in some of the charts you do.

In the natal chart, Saturn signifies the father (along with the Sun), according to Vivian Robson.[16] Saturn is also credited with being the symbol of maturation, responsibility, learning experience, and the crystallization of consciousness. Its interaction with Jupiter creates a balance within the individual, for Jupiterian outreaching needs to be tempered with the saturnine realization of reality. The two energies within us are always at odds, yet they help create our own internal set of checks and balances.

Dal Lee says that it takes Saturn 29.46 years to complete a cycle. This figure actually varies, as you can see from Table 5 on pages 50-51. Because we are working with an average breakdown for the Saturn cycle (with divisions that relate to a 28-year Saturn cycle), it seemed important to show you how the cycle varies when individual birth data is considered. The table shows how the cycles may get off balance, which means that you have to plot the time of the Saturn cycle for each chart in order to know exactly when it will be in effect.

The 28-year cycle breaks down into four seven-year cycles, and the seven-year cycle has been discussed for hundreds of years. We have the seven good years and the seven lean ones, the seven-year itch, and many other kinds of seven-year cycles. All these cycles seem to relate to reaping what we sow or making tremendous changes. They are turning points in life and each phase in the cycle will last about a year.

The Saturn cycle pushes us to grow. The growth will involve the situations in life that need to change in order that we continue on our path to become totally conscious,[17] such as overcoming concepts of restriction, becoming aware of what we know, overcoming fears, coping with feelings of limitation, etc. Every time we go through another Saturn phase, we pull away from our past position, move on to another stage of development and develop strength in some new phase of life. Most of the Saturn energy is geared to teaching us how to approach authority (or natural law) in all its manifestations. The first authority we know is that of our parents. We then move on out into the world and learn to cope with teachers, management, employers, the bully down the street (whether he be 10 or 35), or anything else that we may want to do that doesn't tie in with the present stage of growth.

---

[16]Vivian Robson, *A Student's Text-Book of Astrology*, Cecil Palmer, London, 1922, p. 127.

[17]An interesting discussion of the Saturn bridge to spiritual consciousness may be found in Leo, *Saturn*, Samuel Weiser, Inc., York Beach, ME, 1970. First published in London in 1916.

The outer change caused by Saturn may seem restrictive when we are first learning that we must grow. The world comes and says, "You can't do this." And we don't like it. There is another phase of the Saturn cycle, though, and this is related to the change that takes place on an inner level. It's about knowing what you know, and knowing who you are, and knowing how you fit into your social structure. For example, how are you seen by your employees versus how do you think of yourself? How are you recognized in your field of endeavor? These awarenesses may not be apparent until after the second Saturn return, but they are part of the Saturnian growth pattern.

Saturn stays in a sign for two and a half years, so many people have natal Saturn in the same sign, and many have similar Saturn aspects if they are the same age. The use of Saturn energy is still an individual decision, for the Saturn placement only indicates potential and doesn't guarantee behavior. We all make different choices as to how we want to develop, and these choices relate to the game of chess. Every move you make affects the next one.

We experience three Saturn returns if we live to be 84 years old. A pattern is set in potential when we are born, and we develop more and more responsibility at every hard aspect in the first cycle. At the Saturn return, or the beginning of the second Saturn cycle, we are astrologically adults, having completed all the phases of growing up. The second Saturn cycle is about developing the adult personality and sharing in a larger scope of life. It's the house-holding cycle or the business and career cycle. When the third Saturn return takes place (about age 56), we begin the phase of life having to do with leadership and wisdom. In Western culture this was the phase of the statesman and philosophical leader, who sagely offered advice to younger people. In the East, for the Hindu, it was the time to start reflecting about concepts of spirituality, for the last phase of life has to do with giving up worldly possessions and responsibility to explore the needs of the developing soul.

The ancients said that after three rounds of Saturn life is over, but we know that isn't true because many people live longer. Long life is also attributable to Saturn for this planet has some relationship with longevity and endurance. We will not discuss Saturn stages beyond age 84, for they are out of the scope of this book, and I don't have enough insight to take it that far.

Saturn Cycle 1 (0-28)

The cycle begins at birth. The newborn child is weak and dependent. Years ago when astrologers were questioned about the future of the child, the questions frequently asked were, "Will my child be born alive?" "Will my baby live?" "Will I live through childbirth?"; these were real issues for people at one time. Saturn has something to do with death and finalization, and Saturn's position in relation to the Moon was important in the natal chart. It still is; but because of medical advances, the problems indicated by Saturn may manifest more in relation to psychological effects than physical limitations. At birth, the Saturn placement indicates what the struggle will be about, for hard aspects to Saturn show what the individual will need to overcome during the lifetime. The exact details of the life story are not apparent from the chart, but the cause of the struggle is.

At age seven we experience the first Saturn square. Some people think this is the first time the child learns to submit his ego to the needs of the group, which is certainly something that happens in the school system. The first year of kindergarten, or even first grade, doesn't necessarily inhibit the child from joining his peers. Saturn square itself will usually bring out some behavior that will probably encourage Saturnian discipline. This discipline may be needed because the child is too self-assertive at other children's expense. The child needs to learn he is not alone in the world, that the world doesn't revolve around him, but rather he is a part of it. The child may become aware that the world is full of competition— maybe even war—but the world is definitely not centered around his concept of his needs of the moment. Subjugation of the ego creates a necessary balance in the social structure. We become part of the group and therefore need to have some rules and regulations in common, or we won't have a group. It would be interesting to note how a seven-year-old copes with this experience, because the reaction may be carried into the next Saturn phase.

At age 14 or so, the first Saturn opposition is felt. This part of the Saturn cycle follows behind the Jupiter flowering of the sexual nature. We have adult glands but the mind of a child. Authority is seen as the "enemy," and both parents and teachers are on the "other side." This is when many teenagers get into trouble with the law and end up dealing with police officers. Some boys band together as "outlaws," not in the Robin Hood sense of the word, but in a rebellious sense, as boys undergoing the opposition are anti-authority. Parents are understandably upset during this cycle, as the child is pulling away from them, and may foresake education in the process. On the one hand, the kid needs to pull free, and on the other, the parents are truly concerned with the kid's future.

For young girls, the Saturn opposition follows the development of sexual characteristics, and teenage girls fall in love. This is a rebellious time for girls too, but the rebellion may manifest differently. The biological drive is strong because of the Jupiter cycle, and the Saturn opposition may be the only thing keeping them from becoming involved sexually, as a fear of repercussion (pregnancy) may be sparked by Saturn, at least intuitively. Some girls may start to have sex in response to the Saturn opposition, as this symbolizes becoming a woman to them. While boys are rebellious and need to come up against the father figure in order to establish a separate sense of self, families are worried because they don't know how a young woman will respond to her sexuality and her need to get away from home. The natal chart is very important as far as diagnosing how this cycle will be handled, and it would be handled better by parents who understand that sex is a normal part of life.

At age 21 we experience the second (or final) square in the first Saturn cycle, and this energy often pushes early marriage. Many marry to leave home, driven by a sense of responsibility that sexual development has brought. It may be a marriage that is not carefully thought out, but it is one way to leave home with the approval of family and community, for marriage is a ritual that leads us from one phase of life to the next. Age 21 is important when the Saturn and Jupiter cycles operate at the same time, and we will discuss this again in Part 2.

People who don't marry and start a family at age 21 may do so on other typical marriage years, such as 24 or 28. For some, getting away from home is accomplished by graduating from college, for the young adult leaves school to begin a new career. However it is done, it's important to leave home and learn about living alone. This is sometimes very hard to do, especially when parents have difficulty letting go of their children or the young adult is afraid to leave the nest. Age 21 is a big year, for it means that we are now responsible for our debts, we can enter into legal agreements, and the government considers us old enough to be treated as an adult.

Saturn Cycle 2 (28-56)

The second Saturn cycle begins around the age of 28. Using a ten-degree applying orb we see that this phase of the cycle will be in effect for about a year. The first round of Saturn is complete; we have grown from infant, to teenager, to adult; we have experienced all the things that young adults can experience, such as living alone, being sexual, perhaps being parents, handling responsibility. It's now time to evaluate what we've done and where we are going. This is the astrological cycle that indicates we've come of age.

When Saturn conjuncts itself, it makes for a tremendous year of change, and this is the time to look at where we are going, where we have been, and what future plans will be. The two main issues that need to be handled are career goals and relationships. As Mark Twain said, "When I was 21 my parents were quite ignorant, but by the time I reached 28, they had matured a lot." Obviously he had matured a lot, for he probably was just beginning to understand why his parents responded to life the way they did.

The Saturn return indicates a major readjustment in regard to our philosophy of life. We've established this philosophy quite unconsiously when we were in our teens. It starts like this: "When I get away from home, I will be a such-and-such kind of person. When I am on my own, I won't be like my parents. I will be different." And we leave home, and we're different, and we try to put these ideas into practice. However, the ideas of an idealistic teenager don't always hold water, and we are beginning to realize this. So we are essentially busting up some childhood dreams and concepts that don't work when confronted with reality. This knowledge is painful, as it means we must put away our childish toys and join the ranks of the adults. If we know the cycle is happening, the adjustments are easier to make. If we don't know about the Saturn return, we may feel frustrated because our life plan isn't working so well, or we may feel inadequate for what we've tried to do isn't working and this reflects on our self-image. Losing something on the Saturn return usually happens for a good reason.

Career becomes a big issue. Some people are lucky enough to know what they want to do when they go to college. Others aren't so fortunate. For those who have been unable to get going in a career, this is a time for change. For some, the Saturn cycle indicates a total change in career, for after working for a few years in one field, it may become apparent that this is not what we want to do for the rest of our lives. Decisions made about career on this cycle will usually be good ones, for we are becoming more responsible.

We also consider letting go of certain kinds of permissive concepts that don't relate to the structure of our society. For example: any life philosophy that doesn't hold water or that can't stand the test of time or reality needs to be let go. Morality will be changing. What's that mean? Well, it's nice to be liberal and understanding, but you can get compromised in your own liberality if you don't think about it. Is it really fair that you make your employer be your therapist? Should all employees in the company pull their own weight in relation to the job they hold? Do you still want to cover for Mary or John because they can't do the job? Or, maybe you said that everyone has a right to live the life of their choice. Remember that? Well what happens if you have a couple of kids and you discover that your best friend, who's been hanging out at your house with your kids, is also selling drugs? Want that person around? Suddenly it may be okay to sell drugs as long as people who do it aren't a part of your intimate social circle. Or your responsibility level may change. You may notice that you see your commitments and your responsibilities in a whole new light. The changes can be quite exciting, and by understanding them, you may feel a new security in yourself.

The Saturn return also affects relationships. If you were not married earlier, you may decide that this is an important thing to do. If you don't have children you may decide to have a child on this cycle. If you are unhappily married, you may decide to divorce. The point is that everyone decides to do something. People who don't want to marry may decide to live with someone, or may decide to have more responsible or more serious relationships than they were having before. Both men and women become more definitive about the kind of lifestyle they wish to participate in.

Not everyone wants to become a junior executive in a fast-developing company at the Saturn return. Some people will never have an exciting career, and many don't want one. Some people have several careers, and if this is the case, the Saturn return may mark one of the career changes. These folk are called "Renaissance people" in the trade. They do a number of things well, and the career of the moment is often related to whatever philosophical change is taking place within. On the other hand, some people are on a strongly spiritual trip, and don't want to hold a job that requires a lot of thought or concentration, for the job is only a means to an end. Students of the occult often work in order to buy books, or work to make enough money to study with a teacher. The painter works to buy canvas, and the writer works to pay for the rental of a typewriter for the next book or play. These people are not avoiding the Saturn return; they hear a different drummer, and changes may take place inside instead of outside. The important thing to keep in mind about this cycle is that it indicates a change in maturation.

The second cycle indicates another phase of life. The first one was a building cycle in a personal sense. Can I do this? Can I do that? Now we know we can or can't and it's time to become a person in our own right. The next 28 years essentially encompass all the various stages of being an adult. Forget the mother/father stuff. Anyone, including any teenage child, can make or have a baby. What do we do with it after we have it? We move from biological adult to actually being one. The two squares and the opposition in this cycle indicate stages of growth during the process. And we have very little literature available to teach us how to move through it.

The first square in the second Saturn cycle occurs around age 35. Remember the Jupiter cycle that starts around age 36? The decisions made on the third Jupiter cycle may be influenced by what happens on this first Saturn square. The crisis will relate to a year of re-evaluating plans. The young career person will be assessing whether or not to make a career move. The person involved in career may be bitter about the fact that a career wasn't chosen, or the one that was isn't what is wanted now. The cycle is difficult for young mothers; the conversation you hear from them is, "I'm just a body guard. All I do is shuttle kids from school to football practice. And I even have to take them out on dates!" The mother who says this is not feeling very worthwhile as an individual. It is nice to see little Johnny on the honor roll at school, but she can't live vicariously off her kids if she thinks that she, herself, has something to offer. It's hard at age 35 to consider that the excellent job she does raising her kids will pay off in the future of the social structure. She needs some immediate response and appreciation for the work she does. So the mother has to reassess her values. I usually recommend that she consider part-time work, or work with an organization so that she can re-establish a sense of self-worth.

For the career person, this is a time of re-evaluation as to how you are doing in the career department. If the company doesn't look like it's going to promote you, maybe this is the time to consider a change in jobs. If the move is diagnosed on the Saturn square, maybe the time to do it would be on the next Saturn trine. Or on the new Jupiter cycle coming up.

Saturn is the taskmaster of the zodiac. When we are experiencing trouble on a Saturn cycle square, it usually means that we need to make some adjustments internally. Somehow or another, the decisions and attitudes we've held in the past are outmoded. Saturn energy will bring whatever needs to change to your attention. Usually the problem arises because some authority figure (and in this case, an authority figure is anyone who stands between you and your goal) is giving you a hard time. This is a good time to listen to yourself and analyze what is happening. Granted you may be angry because your superior criticized your work, but maybe you weren't doing what the company needed. Try to get into the larger framework and understand what it is that you are participating in so you can understand what team you are on. It's not you alone against the world; it's you as part of a group.

The square may also signify that it's time to reassess who you are. If you have been a student for a long time, maybe it's now time for you to teach. When will you know that you have learned enough? When can you allow yourself to be qualified enough? Is this an issue? Do you still need to study or do you now have the foundation you need to work with? Who are you becoming in your professional world? Your family? Your town?

This may also be a time to get involved in giving part of yourself to something outside your immediate family and career needs. Maybe offering time to a local organization or your local political group would help. This has to do with building a concept of yourself in a larger scope, broadening your vision outside of just being a worker and a family member. It also allows you to develop fresh insights into yourself, for you meet new people and have to relate yourself to strangers without the crutch of business or family talk.

At approximately age 42, Saturn opposes itself again. This is the next stage up from the opposition you experienced at age 14. It means letting go again, but in a different way. You can't fight your Daddy on this one, so maybe you want to fight the world. If you have worked to develop your career, this opposition should bring some payoffs, and you should see the results of the work you have done. A number of people question decisions made in the past, and this is the time we now call midlife crisis. The chickens come home to roost, they say. Many find this crisis hard to handle.

If your goal was to own the company at age 40 and you don't, you may begin to feel really desperate. Where are you going in this career? Some people feel really self-confident about career, for they've reached the goals they set for themselves, and the crisis is more painful in other areas. Some people become ill, some commit suicide, some leave everything behind and start anew, but this is more associated with the Uranus opposition, which may also be in effect when Saturn's opposition is in.

Many people are disappointed with the achievement they sought, and this realization becomes conscious at the opposition. The phase can also bring us up short when we don't have a concept of who we are, not because we never did, but the concept has to adjust to the life phase we are presently experiencing. The most common problem is that of self-worth as it relates to conscious realization of who we are. Saturn is symbolic of crystallization, of knowing what we know. Well, now it's time to know who you are. Who are you in your community? Your family? What is your new perspective of yourself as a forty-year-old? Granted you may be learning many things in many different areas, but you are also seen by others in a different light. What is this role you play? I'm not talking about a phoney image here, but more about allowing yourself to see you as others do. Many people on a spiritual search don't see who they have become as far as others are concerned, and this is an important step in self-development.

At midlife crisis life is half over. So one of the things you will think about is dying. Maybe a friend dies, and you become acutely aware that life is not permanent. During our 20s and 30s we were primarily concerned with personal accomplishment and developing self. Jupiter is now pushing us to begin to give to and teach others. If we haven't paid attention to the Jupiter cycles, we may suddenly realize that if we don't give some time to friends, family, and loved ones, they might not be there to give to when we finally get around to it.

Relationships were important at the second Saturn return, and they are important again now. Serious thoughts about marriage and family are part of this opposition, for the phase relates to what we did at age 28. This is another time to look at where relationships are going in terms of responsibility. Both the responsibility that you feel and the kind that you expect back. Many parents decide to make more time to spend with each other; some even start taking vacations without the kids so they can get to know each other again. Unmarried people may marry now; some people divorce. How a marriage ends cannot be totally determined upon this Saturn cycle phase, for Uranus is lurking around at the same time and it may be a Uranian decision to marry or divorce rather than one based on Saturn.

The Saturn opposition may be ignored at midlife because the influence of Jupiter, Uranus, and even Neptune can cloud issues relating to Saturn. If aging is seen as something relating to death, and if death is a frightening concept, the healthy side of the aging process may be ignored. If this is the case, the individual may become preoccupied with looking youthful, imitating young people's dress and behavior, thus losing all the satisfaction that could be gained from understanding the maturation process. People who are afraid of dying become preoccupied with health, going on crash diets, trying one health-food fad after another, exercising like crazy, etc. Some people are coping with real health problems now, for Saturn has to do with both long-term illness and longevity, so midlife may also bring on the realization that the Jupiterian overconsumption of junk foods has to go. The values related to the maturation process are important now, for we either walk into the beginning of the second half of our life looking forward to the new experience, or we enter this phase with apprehension and fear. Metaphysically, this attitude is important as it will eventually influence our own aging process.

Seven years later (age 49) we experience the last Saturn square in the second cycle. It happens a year after the fourth Jupiter return. Just as we begin to open up (under Jupiter) to the concept that we need to learn how to accept help graciously, we get tested, for Saturn comes into play. For the next year, Saturn will be testing the decision we made at age 28. The crisis will relate to how we have chosen to live as adults. Career decisions, or family and lifestyle decisions that were put into practice are now being evaluated again. Something about our life is going to resurface, and that "something" needs to be cleaned up on the responsibility level. Age 50 is looming on the horizon. The aging process is setting in. What are we going to do in our older years? We begin to think about what we really want and a lot of people go for it.

This is a rough period for women, for some feel extremely limited if life has been spent completely concentrating on child-raising. The menopause causes a time for reflection, and reflection includes letting thoughts about self-worth come to the surface. If worth has been based only on being a mother, and you no longer can have babies, you have to do something to establish a personal sense of worth that doesn't relate to children. Some women become involved in being grandmothers and even compete with a daughter or daughter-in-law as to who is the better mother. That's not really the best way to handle this energy.

For men, work may be enough to carry them through this period, but on an inner level they know that work will only last for so long. Something is brewing. We intuitively know what's going to happen; the third Saturn cycle is around the corner. The decisions made now will basically affect the aging process and how we decide to handle this experience.

Two things can happen. The rigid Saturnian types get stuck in a rut and try to hold on to what they know. The people who will use Saturnian energy as a part of the learning process will be drawn to experience a new reality. Becoming interested in philosophy, religion, church, or community activities is a key to becoming a part of the process in a constructive way. It's important not to become rigid, and something has to be done to keep rigidity and habit from taking over life. Some people are drawn into metaphysics or the occult at this time, for these studies look at life from a broader perspective. This may be the first time that an individual has considered some form of philosophy, for the earlier years may have been concentrated upon the needs of supporting a family and earning a living.

Saturn Cycle 3 (56-84)

The third Saturn cycle forms the basis for our older years. At age 56 or so, we begin the next phase of life experience, and if we are open to the concept of spiritual development, it indicates the height of human understanding. For those who are religiously or spiritually oriented, the knowledge that the soul lives on forever will lessen the fear of death. For those who feel that life is merely physical, that we have only one shot at living, the fear of death can be quite unnerving, and life becomes something to cling to at any cost.

Men now reconsider where they are heading as far as retirement is concerned, and they need to think about what they want to do for their retirement years. This is a big decision, for in 14 years (age 70 or so) they will be stuck in the decision that is formed now. If retirement is considered the end, then the individual is setting himself up to become old without really allowing for the new growth that can be a delightful part of old age. Many years ago, our statesmen were older men. Today many subscribe to the concept that young people are smarter than wise men, but that is a fad. Those of us who really understand the phases of life can enjoy working with the growth this phase brings.

Women at age 56 are deciding what kind of older women to be. Either they opt for the grandmother role, or they develop into an eccentric personality, or they develop a new career. Yes, career! Many older women become teachers, and the field of astrology is full of women who are sharing their wisdom and knowledge. If personal interests have been given up because the husband and family didn't approve, this is when the woman says, "If you don't like what I'm doing, leave." It's amazing, for the husband usually decides to let his wife pursue her interests at this time. She develops a new strength.

At the beginning of the third Saturn cycle, everyone becomes aware of his or her fallibility. Death also becomes a real part of life, with friends and family leaving the universe, forcing each of us to consider how we want to handle our own inexorable passage into the next world. The issue is a big one for most people, for our culture has not provided much information about the concept of dying except that "Jesus will save you." If we are curious about death, or if we show an interest in the death process, people think we are planning to die. Ridiculous! Birth and death go together. No one is going to get out of this life alive. Elisabeth Kubler-Ross and her work with death and dying has done a great service to the American public for it has made the process a household word.

At the third Saturn cycle we are not necessarily going to die; it's not really part of this cycle! But death is a life event that will become a part of our life experience. Because we are old enough to touch death as a life process, our values will change. We can give with more warmth. We can be supportive of younger people, when before we were concentrating on building our own worth. This is the period for the elder statesman, for the person this age has a lot to offer both company, family, and community. The matriarch and patriarch are developing. Your own parents won't live much longer (if they are still alive), and the third Saturn cycle brings with it the responsibilities of the head of the clan. The tribe or clan equals the family. Do we become doddering and senile? Or do we become the head of the clan as an older and mature advisor?

At this age we can give up the responsibility of being parents in the physical sense of the word. No more ironing and cooking dinner or washing socks. In the Hindu civilization, this is the cycle when you give up household and worldly possessions so you can become an ascetic and develop on a spiritual level. That's because you didn't have time to do it before. Youth is spent being young. Then you become the householder, raise your children, and take care of the needs of your parents. At 56, you get to let your children take care of your needs. This doesn't mean you give up your home and cease to fend for yourself. It means that you cease to take on the responsibilities of your children in the same sense you did before.

This cycle also indicates that it's time to change the concept of who we are. We have been doing for others, building a career and establishing an adult image for the last 28 years. Now we move to the advisory stage, and turn over the hard work to someone younger and less experienced. When this idea is not understood, the older person works even harder to prove that he can still do it, when he doesn't realize that he doesn't have to do it any more. By this age you have proved yourself, and it's time to let go of that kind of a proving process. When this is not understood, and men and women don't step down from one job so thay can enter the next phase, sometimes the job is ripped away from them; they end up being forced out because they couldn't see that they needed to let go voluntarily. The universe is not being unkind, but it is our responsibility to know what to do next and we can't be on the advisory board of the organization if we are still trying to work on the staff. The key here is to discover what it is that we can do to use our knowledge in an advisory capacity and let go of the old ways.

The first square in the third Saturn cycle takes place about age 63, and we test the decision made at the beginning of the cycle. Retirement is coming on for real. This is usually harder on men than on women. Some people may have chosen early retirement at age 60 or 62, and this may be a chance to remake some decisions. Some people decide to go back to work. If they have not become rigid or frightened of the aging process, and if they don't subscribe to the American myth that old people aren't worth anything, this is a satisfying and fruitful period.

The opposition takes place around age 70, bringing the benefits that would be based on the decision made at age 56. If the third Saturn cycle was seen as a new phase to explore in the life process, this should be a pleasant period. If decisions were not well thought out regarding the retirement plan, this may denote the conscious awareness that things should have been done differently. Some people have pulled up and started something else at this age, but that depends on the person. Illness and various stages of ill health may interrupt plans at this time.

If the mind has remained open, and if this cycle has been used to explore the potential of spiritual development, this may be an extremely productive phase. This is the time to write a great book, to do interesting research, to work with life experience and insights gained over the years. In the astrological community we have two great astrologers to look up to—Marc E. Jones wrote books and taught and lectured up until his death, and Dane Rudhyar has over forty books to his credit and is still writing, lecturing, and counseling.

The last square is in effect around age 77, bringing another year of stress. This is a time when people die or watch their friends die, or get ready to do it. Once you get ready to die, you don't have to—it just means that you have made your peace with the idea and it no longer bothers you one way or the other. This can bring increased freedom, for every day is enjoyed to its fullest, and a sunset can really be appreciated for its beauty.

The next Saturn cycle begins around the age of 84, which is the astrologer's end of life. It means that three rounds of Saturn have been completed and we either die or decide to live on. The chances are good that we experience the start of a new Saturn and Jupiter cycle together at this point, which is an interesting concept. Uranus is in there too, in a conjunction to itself. People who opt to live enjoy every day available. Picasso painted to the end. How many others do you know who are still going strong? Usually the people who continue to live have some kind of life's work, something they thoroughly enjoy doing, or they have a life philosophy that allows them to live on for they are at peace with themselves. Hopefully we'll all feel this way, too, because we've worked within the framework of our life cycles and can consequently enjoy living.

CYCLES OF INDIVIDUATION

The three outer planets are considered to be generational planets because everyone born within one generation has the same planet in the same sign. All are somewhat recently discovered, with Uruanus appearing in 1781, Neptune in 1846, and Pluto in 1930. For obvious reasons, astrologers have more to say about Uranus and Neptune than about Pluto since it is still being studied in terms of interpretation.

The cyclic motion of these planets is so vast that we cannot experience a full cycle, but only a portion of it. For this reason, the planets are thought to be symbolic of the energy that lifts us into another plane of consciousness, another realm of being, pulling us away from the merely personal problems of mundane life and forcing us to consider the larger scope of life. We basically are totally self-involved. When litle Johnny goes to school, he has to sacrifice some of his self-centeredness for the consciousness of the group. As we proceed through life, we entertain the idea that other people think and live differently than we do. We sometimes try to live in the narrow confines of our Moon energy, or in the limitations of our Saturn aspects, or whatever planet seems to have the strongest aspects in the natal chart. The outer planets focus our energy into something else; by transit to the personal planets in the chart, they encourage us to change. When they interact in their own cycle, however, the change is much bigger, as these cycles tie into the collective consciousness that is a part of the mass of human life on our planet, allowing some of us to open up and grow beyond the scope of the personal chart. Therefore, they are considered a part of the individuation process, allowing us to get in touch with the Self. The cosmos is the limit.

URANUS CYCLES (84 YEARS)

Jupiter and Saturn cycles used to be the limit for growth. In the 1700s the world opened up. We began to develop a new technology, mastering the art of various types of craftsmanship in a way never before considered. People began to travel and change their way of life. The caste system in the world was beginning to change and people could move from one social position to another. Great devastation was also put upon the world for the spread of disease was rampant for a while. Human slavery became a business like it had never been before, for people were being bought and sold for the sake of the selling, and not because they were victims of war between countries or tribes or because they were poor. Along with all this activity came new attitudes toward people and consciousness, and the discovery of Uranus.

Astrologers disagree about the meaning of Uranus in the personal chart, and each reader will have to determine what Uranus means to him. To some it means revolution, disruption, willfulness, eccentricity, unconventional behavior, stubbornness, rigidity, all the more negative traits of Aquarius.[18] Dal Lee said it indicates individuality and renunciation.[19] To others it means the beginning of the individuation process, for the energy of the planet symbolizes our ability to break the shackles of limitation so we can burst forth with new freedom. When the planet was discovered, rulership was assigned to Aquarius, and Aquarius had been ruled by Saturn up until that time. Saturn is the teacher, and Saturnian energy also relates to our sense of freedom or lack of it. Restriction and limitation are the other side of the coin marked freedom, much like

---

[18]Margaret Hone, *The Modern Textbook of Astrology*, Fowler & Co., Ltd., London, 1951.

[19]Dal Lee, *Dictionary of Astrology*, Paperback Library, Coronet Communications, New York, 1968.

love is the other side of hate, so there is some relationship between Saturn and Uranus.

We may only experience one complete cycle of Uranus in a lifetime, which means it is a much more important cycle than a Mars cycle for instance. If its orbit was dependable we would experience a Uranus change at 21, 42, and 63. The orbit for Uranus is erratic, however, and this means that the timing of the cycle's phases will be affected by individual birth years; the cycle will have to be plotted individually in order to determine the actual stress phases. Table 6 on page 68 shows the Uranus cycle for three different birth years. If you use a ten-degree applying orb to track each phase, you will note that it can be in effect for two to three years, and can, for example, bring on midlife crisis at age 42 or even age 38.

Many astrologers have said that Uranus operates suddenly, out of the blue, fast and quick. It may look that way to others, but I don't think that Uranus decisions are made quickly. The decision has been in the process of being made for some time, and when we finally do something about it, it looks as though we made an emergency decision. We have an even better chance of using the energy well when using a large orb to diagnose it, for instead of having to react to an event in life, we have the opportunity to feel the electrical charges of decision taking place within us, and we can see the seeds of our discontent. I don't think that a teenager will be able to diagnose this energy, but we can use it for midlife crisis and certainly for the last square. Changes made on the Uranus cycle will probably be based on decisions made during various Jupiter and Saturn cycles, as Uranus represents a concept of self that does not emerge overnight.

People who have natal aspects to Uranus involving the personal planets will probably handle these cycles better than people who don't. If you were born with a Moon/Uranus square, Uranus energy will not frighten you. If you were born with a Uranus/Neptune sextile, you may not know exactly how to handle a Uranus transit or cycle, because the flow of energy may be overwhelming, or spark so much excitement that you don't think about what you are doing. Knowing that the energy will be available to use is helpful, for this energy is creative and gives us absolutely brand new ideas about life.

Using the ten-degree applying orb should alleviate most apprehension, for you get a chance to work with the energy at the beginning of the cycle, and have a chance to change your mind and your consciousness. It will come into orb, start the energy flow, and

Table 6. Uranus Cycles and Crisis Years*

Aspect	Average Age	♅ 29° ♓ 53′	Actual Age	♅ 23° ♉ 57′	Actual Age	♅ 25° ♑ 07′	Actual Age
☌	0	Birth	0	Birth	0	Birth	0
□	21	7/20/46-12/9/46 5/9/47-8/27/48 11/16/48-6/8/49	18-21	9/7/58-2/12/59 6/24/59-9/26/60 2/8/61-7/13/61	17-20	10/26/71-5/5/72 8/7/72-11/13/73 5/1/74-8/30/74	16-19
☍	42	9/11/66-9/27/68 5/31/69-6/14/69	38-41	12/5/77-5/15/78 9/23/78-12/30/79 5/5/80-10/17/80	37-39	1/25/92-7/31/92 11/13/92-3/7/94 6/28/94-12/26/94	36-39
□	63	1/8/86-6/24/86 10/28/86-2/12/88 5/30/88-12/1/88	58-60	2/23/99-8/30/99 12/14/99-4/12/01 7/17/01-1/29/02	58-61	5/23/14-9/22/14 3/14/15-4/26/17 11/27/17-2/7/18	58-62
☌	84	3/31/08-10/3/08 1/19/09-5/24/10 8/18/10-3/10/11	80-83	7/5/21-10/5/21 4/20/22-5/28/24 12/20/24-3/12/25	80-83	7/4/36-7/28/38 3/1/39-5/4/39	81-83

*Birth data for Uranus at 29° Pisces 53′ is from 1928; 23°Taurus 57′, from 1941; at 25° Cancer 07′, from 1955. Because of the birth years, the dates for the last square and the conjunction (age 63 and 84) may be in the 21st century. Notice how early the 1928 and 1941 birth dates are through the last square and how the 1955 birth date ends right on the average cycle.

then retrograde back off the natal position for a couple of months. This gives you time to regroup your thoughts. When it returns, you may have two or three bouts with the energy in this two- to three-year period, therefore allowing concepts to develop before you feel moved to take action.

The first square takes place between ages 18 and 21 and we push away from home under this influence. It takes Jupiter, Saturn, and Uranus to get us out of the house. It's not easy to leave the nest, and we are not usually given enough encouragement to get out on our own. Many parents don't realize that the child needs to leave, as leaving is often confused with a loss of love. Some leave home by graduating from college and look forward to starting a new job, maybe living in a new town, or with friends in a nearby city. Others marry and start a new family of their own.

The key to understanding the energy is that it relates to a major change in lifestyle. Depending on other aspects in the natal chart, some young people make good choices and others don't. Some make rash decisions. Most young people will not listen to anything an adult has to say, so intent are they to get out on their own. Some lives are spent trying to repair decisions made on this Uranus square; but no matter what happens, Uranus energy leads us on to the destiny we subconsciously have in mind for ourselves. By destiny I don't mean fate—I mean the subconscious drive that leads us into whatever life experience it is that will help us grow in the direction the soul chooses.

The opposition takes place between the ages of 38 and 42, again combining with a Jupiter and Saturn cycle, and sometimes Neptune square Neptune. The more cycles in effect during this period, the more oppressive the energy; it is easier to handle the various cycles if they come in at different times. When they are all happening at once, you are going to make profound changes. If this is the case, it's worth knowing about the pressure you are under, so hopefully you can make better moves.

Uranus has been called the symbol of willfulness, eccentricity, and unconventional behavior. At midlife crisis, the Uranus energy may present itself as an electric, erratic force, pushing us to find and face ourselves. If we have chosen a placid marriage and that is not what we want any longer, we may divorce. If we have chosen a career that is unfulfilling, the Uranian energy helps us become aware that we need to change. If we are outer-directed, event-oriented personalities, we will try to change our environment. If we are more inner-directed people, we will know that the dissatisfaction with the outer environment relates somehow to changes that need to take place on an inner level. How we use this energy is up to us.

Uranus says, "I'm not getting anywhere. I want to change my life. I'm not getting any younger. I want my youth back. Why did I spend all those years working for my wife and kids out in suburbia when I'm not really enjoying it? Life isn't meaningful. My job isn't meaningful." And so off with one wife and one family, and off with the old job and on to another. Women do the same thing from the other side of the coin. Bored with life, bored with kids and husband, they divorce and run away with some ne'er-do-well looking for excitement, only to learn they haven't found excitement at all. Again, outer-directed changes can be made, but not at the expense of avoiding taking a look at inner-level changes.

A typical example of Uranus influence on midlife crisis is the following: A college professor decided that his life was a bore. He was married and had two teenage kids. He left his wife and family and married an 18-year-old girl. One last fling. His wife hated him and his kids disowned him. She thought he was wonderful. She dated him while he was still married and making a decent living. After he married her, he decided to change careers as well as wives and took a drop in salary in order to get a new job in a new field. He discovered she was pregnant. They could no longer go out after the baby came, for he had to pay alimony, child support, and cope with the expenses of a new baby and a new household on a low salary. She was bored. She left. She also left the baby. He was left standing in the middle of his apartment saying, "What happened?" He didn't really know. But he did take all his inner dissatisfactions and try to project them out on the universe instead of cleaning up what needed to be cleaned up inside.

He could have talked about his dissatisfactions with his first wife. She liked him, and his kids liked him. He was really not unhappily married; he was really bored. He really didn't want to run around with a sweet young thing on his arm; he couldn't keep up with her energy and he didn't care for her interests. The career could have changed with his first wife's support, but if all that would have happened, you wouldn't be reading this story. Uranus influences us to throw out the baby with the bath water. A complete change, says Uranus. We don't have to do that.

Midlife crisis reflects a need to make major changes in life, but these changes can be ones that last. The need for change reflects a need to express yourself differently. You need to change, but you can use what you've learned in a different way rather than throwing all your life experience away and starting from scratch.

Some people want to make career changes on this cycle, and that's fine as long as the new career is somewhat related to past experience. You can't go from running a garment business to owning a hotel in the country if you don't have any experience in running a hotel or living in the country. You can, but how much do you want to learn the hard way in your 40s? The *decision* to go into something new may come to you abruptly. Why can't you discuss it with your mate? The worst that could happen is that she or he doesn't understand what you want to do. If that's the case, then that has to be worked out. If you are married or living with someone who feels inconvenienced because you need to change your work, then it's time to re-evaluate the whole relationship because something major is wrong here.

If your wife says you can't quit your job and move to Idaho because Susie has to finish school in East Podunk, Ohio, she's using that for some kind of a cop-out to moving. Many things have to be considered when you want to change lifestyles in midstream. But they can work, and many people have worked this out constructively.

The person who runs into midlife crisis willing to change, willing to keep on running with this new phase of life, may also be brought up abruptly. One of the issues of midlife crisis is life itself. Hence the high suicide rate at this time. Jumping into or out of something can cause one to think that jumping out of life is one way to handle a crisis, but it isn't. Deciding that your life is a failure because it isn't what it's cracked up to be isn't the answer either. The Uranus opposition brings with it a reality that many of us aren't prepared to face.

The first square happened around age 21, remember? It was a rash breaking away from home. "I'll be a person," you said. "I'll be better than my parents. I'll be important." Well, what's important? At the opposition, Uranus says to you, "Well, you're still not free. You're still not an individual." You end up realizing that you still have some growing to do, and you aren't as mature as maybe you thought you were. You can still be drawn up short. As a matter of fact, you've been so busy proving yourself in the universe that you haven't really taken the time to be yourself. Now what does that lead to? It certainly doesn't do much for one's self-esteem. But the way to get self-esteem is not to run away from everything you've been.

Perhaps you could walk away, knowing that the next phase of your individuation process is at hand. The future you build for yourself now will have a very different value structure than the previous one, because you are on a different end of the Uranus cycle.

Some find it disconcerting to discover they have hit the midway mark in life. This brings the concept of death into view, and many people get a firsthand experience with death. Someone they love dies, or a family member dies, or they themselves get sick enough to have to face up to the reality that life doesn't last forever. That either forces us to reconsider the meaningfulness of our lives, or it makes us scared, so we need to run, run, run to make sure that we get all the life that's due us. As you can surmise, this is the aging youth you see running around the resorts today—Dapper Dan and Dapper Dora, trying to reach back to a vanishing youth.

The marvelous thing that we get as a result of midlife crisis is the appreciation of life. We get a shove from the universe and become aware of how precious the living experience can be, and we have enough experience under our belts to enjoy it like no 20-year-old can. Youth is wasted on the young so they say. And it is.

At age 63 or so, we experience the last square of Uranus to itself and this one ushers in a new phase in the individuation process. Saturn may be square Saturn, Jupiter may be square Jupiter, and if they are, the cycle is a high-pressure period. Not only is this the retirement age for real, but it is a time when a lot of people unconsciously stop living. I'm not talking about death, but an inner decision that is made to give up. We may eventually become ill, lose our sight or hearing, become totally dependent, actually give up on enjoying life. Part of this decision may derive from a lack of self-worth, because the individual bought into the youth syndrome so prevalent in our culture. But we may have also bought into the Mommy/Daddy syndrome, feeling that our usefulness is over. There are other states of being, and childbearing is not the only thing one can do in life. The choice is up to you.

Another option of this cycle would be to encourage the development of the last stage of individuality. This development takes place if the individual is willing to consider philosophical or religious development which will also include looking at the concept of death. The coward dies a thousand times. The fear of death is a horrible thing to live with, as it promotes a constant fear of life. This closes the mind and makes the world appear to be dangerous. The person closes off in an attitude of self-protection. Locked doors, don't go out at night, don't do this, don't do that, don't go here, don't enjoy. Taking religious classes, joining in a psychological or spiritual retreat, taking a workshop or a spiritual development course, or investigating any aspect of the occult sciences can open new doors to living. This kind of openness can completely change your concept of individuation, bring out the process of the soul. It's called knowing where you stand. This is the phase of life that is geared to becoming the wise old woman or the wise old man, and can be the start of a glorious twenty-year period.

NEPTUNE CYCLE (164.8 YEARS)

As you can see, the cycle of Neptune is roughly 165 years, and is therefore one that we cannot consider really personal. It does affect us, however, especially when it ties into the same time frame as other cycles. Table 7 on page 74 shows the years of cyclic activity in the Neptune orbit, and you will note that Neptune square Neptune will have to be plotted individually in order to determine the exact time of its occurrence. It doesn't have as erratic an orbit as Pluto, as you will see when you read the next section.

There are varying opinions about the meaning of Neptune in the natal chart, and your decision about what the planet symbolizes will determine how the cycle works for you. Dal Lee said Neptune was the planet of supermentality, that it is mystical, introspective, religious, on the one hand, and melancholy, morbid, and unreliable on the other. It relates to inspiration.[20] Margaret Hone defined Neptune as a planet that represents formlessness, intangibility, and assigned spirituality to it. She said it is a key to understanding the ability to dissolve the bonds of the material world, and represents inspiring urges from the intangible, which seem to come from the unconscious.[21] In a lecture given in the early 1970s, Lionel Day said that Neptune symbolizes the ideals and dreams of a generation, and other astrologers have said that it symbolizes dream goals in the personal chart.[22]

---

[20]Dal Lee, *Dictionary of Astrology*, Paperback Library, Coronet Communications, New York, 1968.

[21]Margaret Hone, *The Modern Textbook of Astrology*, Fowler & Co., Ltd., London, 1951.

[22]For a complete volume devoted to natal Neptune and its transits, see *The Neptune Effect*, Patricia Morimando, Samuel Weiser, Inc., York Beach, ME, 1979.

Table 7. Neptune Cycles and Crisis Years*

Aspect	Average Age	Ψ 28° ♌ 48'	Actual Age	Ψ 25° ♍ 46'	Actual Age	Ψ 25° ♎ 48' R	Actual Age
☌	0	Birth	0	Birth	0	Birth	0
□	42	12/14/64-5/3/65 10/18/65-12/1/69 6/18/70-9/30/70	36-42	2/10/77-4/25/77 12/6/77-7/30/78 9/26/78-1/18/82 6/14/82-11/22/82	35-41	2/17/91-6/22/91 12/21/91-1/31/96 8/9/96-12/1/96	36-41
☍	84	3/21/06-7/28/06 1/21/07-2/28/11 9/19/11-12/29/11	79-83	4/27/18-8/12/18 2/24/19-4/2/23	77-82	4/18/32-11/2/32 2/15/33-5/26/36 10/6/36-3/27/37	77-82

*Neptune at 28° Leo 48' is from a 1928 birth date; at 25° Virgo 46', from 1941; at 25° Libra 48', from 1955. Note the difference between the "average" cycle and when it actually happens. Depending on birth years, dates in this table include both the 20th and the 21st centuries.

The planet remains in one sign for about 14 years, so many people have Neptune in the same sign. It can hardly be considered personal, but it certainly can be thought of as a representative of the ideals, dreams, and mystical interests of a generation of people. Individuals will react to different manifestations of the energy. Everyone has the option to develop spiritually, and if we use the Neptune energy to tap into the creative source within us, we can work in an extremely creative way. If we have aspects between personal planets and Neptune in the natal chart, we can either express some of that creativity, or we can be used by it in some way. All Neptunian types have a choice whether to develop creativity or to wallow in the mist of delusion, avoiding the harsher realities of life that are usually assigned to Saturn. In order to develop consciousness to its fullest potential, we need to recognize the interplay between Saturn and Neptune. Mystical concepts are important, but we must also survive. We can be purely mystical only when we are completely taken care of, and that idea doesn't work really well in our society in this day and age.

To digress a moment: If you compare Saturn and Neptune it should be done in perspective. The high side of Neptune is spirituality, knowing and understanding the more mystical side of life. The high side of Saturn symbolizes the understanding of form and manifestation. You can't compare Neptune's creativity with the personal limitation or rigidity that Saturn may manifest in an individual. Neptune in its spiritual sense must be compared to Saturn in its spiritual sense, or with Saturn's relationship to the life/death process. Saturn has been called the Grim Reaper, so the planet symbolizes the end of life. If we are going to compare the restriction and self-limitation symbolized by Saturn energy in a personal sense, then we have to compare it to the more personal characteristics of Neptune, the maya of unreliability or illusion/delusion. Maya is not creative, nor is it spiritual. It is merely delusion, and is similar in type to the lower forms of Saturn expression. I say this because some people think that Saturn is a "low" planet vibrationally in the horoscope. It isn't. Saturn is the structure.

During a lifetime, we should be able to incorporate the mystical concepts of Neptune with the personal concepts of individuation signified by Uranus, and then move to dissolve the bonds of reality by participating in the new birth that Pluto symbolizes. In the lifetime of the soul, that can be a grand accomplishment. How often do we have a chance to use Neptune energy? Not often, for we are usually too afraid of the spiritual concepts that underlie the energy of the cycle. We cover it over and prefer to see Neptune as a planet of misinformation. The orbits of Uranus and Pluto are the ones that are changing the most quickly at this time, so they probably indicate the need of the world soul at the moment. In time this may change, but we have been involved in this new development of consciousness for only two hundred years. Some call this the Aquarian Age and say that the changes taking place indicate that humankind as a group is not yet ready to relate to the highest side of Neptune.

The Neptune cycle allows spirituality or the concept of spiritual development into the consciousness around the time of midlife crisis. It also allows us to escape from life if we wish to do that. It takes the soul on a different trip. At the end of life, Neptune energy can open the door to further inspiration if one particpates in religious rituals so that the purpose of their structure can be understood. Once the structure is understood, it is no longer needed, and Neptune dissolves again.

The first square will come into sight between ages 36 and 42. Very few people will notice this energy when using a ten-degree orb, for Neptunian influence is very subtle. If Neptune symbolizes an inner quest for spirituality, Neptune square Neptune will obviously be ignored by many. The energy will intensify as it gets closer to the exact square, and when Neptune is three or four degrees away from the exact square, it will be quite obvious, as obvious as Neptune can get. One of the key words is *dissolving,* so Neptune is a solvent of some kind. It takes away whatever needs to be taken away, and you may not really notice what's happening.

If part of yourself is dissolving, that can be quite a frightening experience, for something has changed that you realize you don't really control with your conscious mind. At this time, you are undergoing some phase of midlife crisis, and many other bonds are being dissolved, bringing a lot of unrest and instability. Most Westerners are uncomfortable when they aren't sure of the future, so this is a feeling that may not be discussed. In the counseling process, I notice that Neptune elicited some of the most interesting responses when counseling its transits and cycles because I could open up a discussion of something the client was afraid of. Usually Neptune is so subtle that the individual who is not in a tightly knit spiritual program may begin to doubt his or her sanity.

If Neptune symbolizes the ideals of the generation you were born into, and if it also symbolizes the barely conscious dreams for society that were prevalent when you were born—ideals and dreams that were not wholly conscious but that were absorbed from the fabric of the atmosphere of the sign Neptune was in—when this concept begins to change, it can shake the very foundations of the personality. It rocks the foundation because it is unmentionable. We can cope with what we can talk about, but as Jung said, when unconscious contents of the psyche are not recognized, or when certain facets of personality are repressed, the energy can begin to take on a strength and life of its own. This could be true of the Neptune placement as it relates to the "great dream of the generation," and when the dream starts to fade, or if the dream fails, the new reality can be very disturbing.

If natal Neptune aspects personal planets in the chart, when transiting Neptune squares itself the activities and dreams of the generation become much more personal. Personal failure could be an issue, for Neptune is influencing other parts of the personality. For anyone with strong Neptune configurations in the natal chart, this is a time of renewal. New goals have to be established. The goals and dreams of the generation, and therefore your response to the needs of your generation, are in the process of change. This is the beginning of the first half of old age. It's a learning period. Usually the minor goals that were set (Saturn-oriented goals) have been achieved at midlife, and a whole new set of values needs to be determined.

By resetting goals, I'm not talking about when you will buy a new car or where you will move. I'm talking about the much more vague goals and dreams of knowing, seeing, becoming conscious of whatever it is you wish to pursue. Usually the first half of life is tied to accomplishments of one kind or another. The second half of life needs to start the beginning of quite a different search.

The Neptune opposition to itself takes place around the age of 82. If 84 is the astrologer's end of life, then the Neptune opposition is a kind of forerunner to the death process. Neptune symbolizes dissolution, and another change in spiritual consciousness. It could be used merely to hurry up the death process, but it seems that the opposition could also signify another breakthrough to consciousness of the meaning of life.

People going through this cycle should be encouraged to participate in meaningful religious rituals. It doesn't matter whether or not you belong to a church group, or if you create one of your own. The symbolism of any spiritually oriented group should enhance the possibilities for further insight. The unsettling side effects of Neptune will probably be more apparent in those who have no spiritual beliefs, and Neptune will pull at the strings of credibility, leaving a bleak future for the person who has no philosophy. Counselors are in an excellent position to help during this period. Any metaphysical training, any experience with hospice in your hometown, or with any organization geared to the crises of spiritual consciousness will help you develop understanding of this part of life.

It has not been my experience to do much counseling with people at this age. For the few clients that fit this age bracket, the questions were about death. And work. And the meaning of life. However, all the people who discussed this with me were involved in spiritual development already, and had reached some under-standing. Ironically enough, all the people I talked with were also still working in some way!

PLUTO CYCLE (248 YEARS)

Obviously we are not going to experience too many phases of the Pluto cycle in one lifetime! If it takes Pluto 248 years to go around the Sun, according to the scientists that have plotted Pluto's course, then you should be approximately 62 years old when you experience the first Pluto square. Not so. Pluto's motion is erratic. In Table 8 on page 80, you will see three different Pluto positions calculated for three different birth years. One person experiences the square of Pluto to itself between September 1974 and September 1978, or between the ages of 46 and 50. Another will experience it between the ages of 40 and 45, while the youngest will cope with it between ages 33 and 38.

To see if the Pluto cycle would change for the opposition (we should live so long), I checked the birth data in Table 8 in a 21st century ephemeris and discovered that for the person born in 1928, the Pluto opposition would happen between ages 83 and 88 if you use a ten-degree applying orb. For the 1942 birth data, the opposition is in effect between ages 78 and 84, while the 1955 birth data has Pluto in opposition to itself between ages 77 and 82! This is a long way from the 124-year opposition that relates to the 248 year cycle.[23] Something is happening in our world. It must be something

---

[23] If you want a fast reference to Pluto cycles (the sextile and the square), see Mary Vohryzek's article "Power and Choice" in the 1983 December National Astrological Society's Newsletter. Available from the society, c/o Barbara Somerfield, 205 3rd Ave., New York, NY 10003.

related to taking the cork out of the bottle called consciousness. Or maybe it's called Pandora's box.

What does Pluto mean to you in the natal chart? To some it means the unconscious motivations and drives of a generation, because many people are born with Pluto in the same sign. Some feel it ties us to the collective unconscious. It could symbolize the subconscious drive for rebirth and transformation that is involved with the process of individuation as it is described by Jung. It could symbolize life itself, as Shiva does when he dances his dance of life and death, constantly dancing through all forms and manifestations of life, just dancing on and on. To many astrologers, Pluto means a drive for power, manipulation and control, which indicates either massive energy being applied for the common good, or massive energy being applied to the common bad. Contacts with the underworld, labor movement, tremendous unrest, unseating the old ways in order to give birth to the new. Whatever the planet symbolizes to you will be how it works for you in the cyclic process. If you're not sure what it means, you may discover new meaning for it as you personally experience the energy in your own life. I'm sure that as more and more astrologers work with the energy, and watch it operate in the universe, we will have more detailed information to work with in future years. We've been studying Pluto effects for only fifty years and more information will come from those who are born knowing the planet exists, who go through a lifetime with it and experience all the possible types of transformations.

If Pluto is considered to represent the collective consciousness, or the collective unconscious, it will have tremendous effects on society as a whole, with some personal effect on those able to grasp its power. But its power must be formidable if it represents all people everywhere. If it symbolizes the collective unconscious, then we are talking about stuff that Jung said would never surface. These are all the tribal memories that have existed in mankind since prehistoric times. If Pluto represents the collective consciousness, then it represents the hope of humanity, for it means that the species is capable of attaining heights of consciousness that are indescribable now, for we are not there yet. The last several hundred years have brought more opportunities for more people have choices about their futures, more people are aware of the brotherhood of the entire planet, more people are realizing that you can't hate the people in the next country for the earth has become too small. In all of this chaos and turmoil, Pluto is working to bring something to light. Maybe to bring us back to the source of all of philosophical and religious teachings—that we are all brothers and sisters. Once that is

Table 8. Pluto Cycles and Crisis Years*

Aspect	Average Age	♇ 16° ♋ 0' R	Actual Age	♇ 2° ♌ 02'	Actual Age	♇ 24° ♌ 27'	Actual Age
♂	0	Birth	0	Birth	0	Birth	0
□	62	11/16/73-3/6/74 9/12/74-12/3/77 3/10/78-9/26/78	45-50	10/23/80-5/19/81 8/13/81-1/17/84 2/22/84-10/24/84 6/22/85-8/1/85	39-44	12/28/88-4/10/89 10/22/89-12/27/92 5/4/93-10/23/93	33-38
☍	124	1/21/11-7/4/11 11/24/11-1/30/16 7/14/16-12/4/16	83-88	2/14/19-7/8/19 12/21/19-4/18/24 5/18/24-1/31/25	78-84	3/17/32-7/17/32 1/23/33-10/13/33 11/11/33-3/8/39	77-84

*Pluto at 16° Cancer 02' is from 1928; at 2° Leo 02', from 1942; at 24° Leo 27', from 1955. The Pluto cycle seems to be really changing. As you can see the first square should take place at 62 and is now taking place between the ages of 33 and 50, while the opposition is taking place between the ages of 77 and 88 rather than at the 124 years that would divide the cycle in half! Dates listed are from both the 20th and 21st centuries depending on birth years.

realized, maybe we will be able to advance to new depths of communication, with ourselves and with the cosmos.

In the meantime, in the midst of each very personal Pluto square itself, the individual will find himself or herself pushed into a new state of being. The only thing that can be said about Pluto square Pluto as a cycle is that we can't control it. Studying astrology to know what will happen won't help, because the best laid plans will be "plutonized." The cycle seems to pull us up from our roots, from our heredity, from our expectations. It can whirl us into another life experience, and we find ourselves doing something else without even knowing we planned to change.

Other people fight their way through the Pluto square, trying to hold their ground, not letting go, fighting to hang on to the past. Some succeed fairly well, from what I can see, for they are not moved to change. Others become locked into a certain kind of hopelessness, fearing to confront the bogeyman inside for fear of what might come up. I've seen people completely removed from previous life experience. In several cases, relationships have changed drastically. Normally this person would not end a relationship or a marriage because of family ties to relatives, children, the neighborhood, and what is known and comfortable. But I have counseled people who have been catapulted into divorce under very strange circumstances, where neither partner really knew what happened, except at the end it was over, and it was like the relationship had never happened. In another case, the individual lost a mate through death and suddenly found herself doing work she had never done before, going from the materialistic world of suburbia and too much alcohol to becoming a dedicated member of the healing profession. Some have become involved in hospice or spiritual development after experiencing the Pluto square. A total change in values can take place.

The square unseats us, for we do not know where we stand. We may find ourselves doing something in which we had no previous interest, or setting up a completely different lifestyle to what we expected. Sometimes I wonder if the Pluto square is really personal. For example, President Nixon was unseated via the Watergate situation while experiencing the Pluto square Pluto.

Nixon has Pluto at 28° Gemini, and dealt with Pluto square Pluto from April of 1967 until September of 1971. The cycle didn't end in September because his natal Pluto also opposed Mars at 29° Sagittarius, with Mercury at 0° of Capricorn and Jupiter at 1° Capricorn. So the energy didn't leave him until mid-September 1972. He had one more brief bout with it in June of 1973, but by then the Watergate issue was settled. I'm not trying to say that the Pluto cycle was responsible for the Watergate situation, but it could be that the stress and uncertainty of the Pluto square caused some of the insecurity that made him respond to life the way he did at that time. For those interested in looking at the incident more completely, you may want to read the discussion in Rob Hand's *Planets in Transit*.[24] I bring up the chart to point out that underlying energies activated during such a cycle may not be used very well. No one transit or cycle *makes* us fall apart, but the energy can be influential in not-well-thought-out behavior when it involves any outer planet cycle.

On the other side of the coin, maybe we aren't supposed to use the energy well. Maybe we get hooked into a plan that makes us grow, whether we are ready or not. In Nixon's case, his personal trauma affected all of us, bringing a new consciousness up from the depths and involving all people—Americans and citizens of other countries in the world. He may have been a martyr to the development of another consciousness, much like Judas was to Christianity. One of the stories, by the way, is that Judas was picked by Jesus to betray him. And Judas' response to being picked was to say, "Master, why me?" The story is credited to the Pluto-ruled sign of Scorpio, for Judas is sometimes described as one. This certainly does relate to the transformation and rebirth syndrome, for if Jesus couldn't die, he couldn't be reborn.

The opposition that is not supposed to happen until the present generation is 124 years old will be happening along with the beginning of the second Uranus cycle. We have no information as to how this energy will manifest. If 84 is the astrologer's end of life, and if a Pluto cycle is present when death should be a subject of interest, it is noteworthy that this present generation is concerned with death education. As soon as we can be less afraid of the word death, we can live the end of our lives very differently, and with a different cause. It remains up to all of us to observe how this energy will work in our lives.

[24]Robert Hand, *Planets in Transit*, Para Research, Rockport, MA, 1976.

PART 2

THE CRISIS YEARS: AGES AND STAGES

Tis not the mere stage of life but the part
we play thereon that gives the value.

J.C. F. von Schiller
Fiesco

No matter how much astrology we know, and no matter what else we know, we can't avoid experiencing cycles. Life begins when we are born, and we continue to grow until we die. If we can understand that growth is a normal ongoing process, we can harness the energy of our growth cycles and use that energy to enrich our life experience. As soon as we understand that cyclic growth is inevitable, the knowledge of upcoming periods of stress enables us to avoid the shock and trauma that can occur when we are totally unprepared for the next step in our lives.[1]

Before exploring each crisis period in depth, we need to look at the concept of crisis itself. The word means that we have reached a juncture, that a decision is going to be made during this crisis, and the decision we make will affect the rest of our lives. In our present society, the word has taken on a different connotation, as to some people it implies a situation than cannot be handled alone. Crisis counseling has been considered a kind of therapy used when an individual can't handle an immediate life situation. To consider this implication even further, many people feel that a crisis is something dire, life-threatening, or a word that implies some kind of failure. The definition of crisis used in this book is the first one mentioned—it's an important decision-making time.

In a major decision making crisis, people sometimes feel fearful. The fear associated with a life crisis is probably best defined

---

[1] Normal crisis periods should not be confused with a traumatic event. Totally traumatic events are those we are completely unprepared for, such as the loss of a loved one by accident or illness, a major accident, terrible fires, etc. These kinds of events are not related to what we are discussing here. However, if a major event occurs during the middle of a normal crisis cycle, the pressure may be extremely difficult. A client coming to talk about a traumatic event doesn't need to hear about his cycles!

as a fear of change. We seldom like to admit that we are still closely tied to the family unit of our youth, but many adults are; they fear change when it relates to the unfamiliar. The root of the word *familiar*[2] is tied to the family, which means we are essentially still rooted in our families in our psyches, whether we stay close to the family or not. We are willing to change when we are children, but something interferes when adults are required to change.

Exploring the idea of childhood changes versus adult changes, let's look at the myth of our adult existence for a minute. When we are born we are totally dependent, yet we reach out with fingers and toes to search out the world around us. We move from the crib to the floor and we eventually explore what's in the cupboard under the kitchen sink. We try walking and running, and we are essentially learning something new every day for the first four years of life. When we enter the school system, we begin another learning procedure, one in which most children are graded. We either pass or fail, and we become aware of our limitations because our weaknesses may be pointed out more often than we are praised for what we've done well. When we graduate from school, we somehow think that we have now reached adulthood, and with adulthood comes the implication that we are through growing. Here starts the problem. Most people are not prepared for the normal changes that adults experience because we are seldom taught that these changes will occur. We wander blithely down the path of life, not really planning ahead, not ready for the changes in consciousness that are inevitable.

Recently our society has become aware that adults change and grow during their entire lifetime, and a great deal of literature is now being published about the stages of life. I feel that Jungian psychology has been very important to the development of this concept because Jung advocated counseling patients in the realm of the search for individuation, rather than only counseling neurotic types. In the last twenty years, we have begun to talk about midlife stress as a crisis, and Elisabeth Kübler-Ross has done a great deal of work to help us become comfortable with the process of death and dying, which is another major crisis that had been ignored.

This section describes crisis by ages so the reader can quickly refer to stress years of interest and see the probable phases in astrological cycles that will be in effect at that time. You will note

---

[2]*Familiar* is a word that means "of or pertaining to the family; domestic." My definition comes from *Webster's New Collegiate Dictionary*, 2nd Edition, G. & C. Merriam Co., Springfield, MA, 1958, p. 208.

that I've pointed out the basic trauma, and some of the ways the energy manifests when it is misused or misunderstood. I have not done a lot to counsel what steps should be taken except in a very general sense, for these steps should be determined by the symbolism of the natal chart for the individual in question. An inner voice speaks to us during times of crisis, and as long as the voice is communicating something constructive, it probably is a good one to follow.

Age 0
Birth

Yes, birth *is* a crisis! Being born is quite a traumatic event, for both mother and child. Being able to survive the trauma of birth itself ought to help some of us understand that we can also survive other crises, *not* because of anything we do, for it just happens. Jung said that the most important crises in life are often just *lived through*, and when we counsel others maybe we ought to keep that in mind.

Age 2-3
First Jupiter Square Jupiter (First Cycle)

We are learning how to eat, walk, talk, hear, see, learn, and absorb from the universe. The first Jupiter square pushes us from the crib into the kitchen cabinets, and eventually into the backyard. Jupiter inspires us to relate to the universe and we absorb everything in a totally self-centered fashion. We begin to move from being totally dependent to being independent. We reach out with our newfound arms and legs. Our mothers are not always pleased at this stage as our Jupiterian exuberance often creates quite a mess!

Age 5-8
Jupiter Opposite Jupiter (First Cycle)
First Saturn Square Saturn (First Cycle)

Hopefully these two cycles won't occur at the same time. If they do, the child experiences a lot of pressure, causing Mom and Dad a lot of grief. The child is now pushed to the next stage of development, which usually takes place at school. On the one hand, the child reaches out to peers (Jupiter) and on the other, his reaching isn't being totally accepted. He wants to relate on his level, and the opposition of Jupiter to itself says that he must compromise in some way. Mom let him destroy the kitchen cabinets at age three, but little

Mary next door will not let him take all her toys or have his way all the time.

The first Saturn square to itself indicates that the teacher (the tester, the voice of law and authority) will not approve of everything the child attempts to do. Law and order in the classroom, learning to play by the rules, doing things he doesn't want to do, these are issues.

Some parents find this a difficult period; they want to support the child's inquisitiveness but also have to support the reality that we live in a social group. This part of the cycle teaches the child he must conform to the group in some respects, he must live by some social rules, and he will not always get his own way in the group. This is the first experience of subjugation of the ego. Many of the lessons are learned away from home: the teacher is a stranger, the rest of the kids in class are the child's peers. Mom isn't there to understand.

This phase of the cycle also may indicate the child's first awareness of separation from the parent. He can still run home for protection, but he doesn't have the feelings of dependency that he had before. This age was once the beginning of a child's working career. I would imagine work in this case would be tied to the symbolism of the Saturn square Saturn.

Age 8-9
Last Jupiter Square Jupiter (First Cycle)

The next push in the relating cycle is that of establishing friendships with peers while relating less to Mom and Dad. It's another push toward independence. Peers are important; group behavior is important. The child is "very grown up" now and can take care of himself. Because it's important to be a grown-up, you'll note the child imitating Mom or Dad's behavior and becoming a sort of mirror image of one of the parents. The child begins to play a role, imitating adult roles as he or she sees them.

Some of the pressure of this cycle occurs because the parents are unprepared to let go of the child. The child is beginning to grow away from them and this cycle indicates both physical and mental growth, the development of physical and mental agilities. Perhaps this cycle is more difficult for mothers to manage because, up until this point, the child has been dependent on her. Now she sees him going out on his own, and sometimes it's hard to let go.[3]

---

[3]See *Child Behavior*, F. Ilg and L.B. Ames, Perennial Library, Harper & Row, New York, 1955, for more discussion of childhood responses.

Age 11-12
Jupiter Conjunct Jupiter (Second Cycle)

The first Jupiter cycle concerned physical growth. It was about relating to arms and legs and baseball or dolls. This second cycle is concerned with the next phase of human development, that of developing sexually so the child can eventually become a parent. We don't like to admit that we are an animal species, but our bodies are whether we admit it or not. Males are made to be fathers and females are made to reproduce the species. The physical development process makes that quite clear![4] The cycle symbolizes a crisis, for each child now experiences a change in the body. Girls develop breasts (or not) and begin to menstruate (or not). Much of the trauma involved with this second Jupiter cycle is caused by the peer pressure brought on by either developing ahead of the crowd or behind it. If the young girl is not lovingly trained by her mother, she can develop phobias about the natural functions of her body—a typical one being disgust in regard to the menstrual cycle. In some cultures, stress is lessened because the young girl experiences a puberty rite, and her psyche knows she has changed. Contemporary Jews celebrate the bas mitzvah, which seems to now be merely a social event for young girls. I'm not sure if the source of this contemporary ritual is based on an older and more meaningful one.

For both men and women, the rite of passage is important, as Joseph Campbell indicates when he talks of the male rite of circumcision. He says that the prime function of mythology and ritual is to supply the necessary symbols to lead the human spirit into the next stage of life.[5] Initiation into adulthood is also discussed by Esther Harding, and she says that ritual experienced in order to become a member of the tribe breaks a certain childish dependence on the family, bringing each young person into the consciousness of a group affiliation.[6] In some cultures (especially among the Spanish) young girls celebrate the arrival of the first menstrual cycle. They are given presents by other women in the family, and are now allowed to listen in on women's conversations, because when menstruation begins, the young girl has become a woman herself.

---

[4]I am not talking about sexuality here; I am talking specifically of the functions of the physical organs present in every human body.

[5]See *The Hero with a Thousand Faces*, Joseph Campbell, Bolligen Series XVII, Pantheon Book, Inc., New York, 1961, pp. 10, 11; and *Myths to Live By*, The Viking Press, New York, 1972.

[6]See *Psychic Energy: Its Source and Its Transformation*, M. Esther Harding; Bollingen Series X, Pantheon Books, New York, 1963, p. 92.

According to Harding, young boys are initiated into tribal secrets "after which they are received into full membership in the tribe." The Jupiter cycle, then, is symbolic of the changing role that is ahead for the child. It is another phase of the separation from the parent, and a time to begin to consider living as an adult. It has, of course, its pitfalls, for one must cope with the unfamiliar, and move one more step away from the family nest, developing the sexual characteristics that determine the survival of the species.

Each child responds differently to the second Jupiter cycle: some become "big babies" for a while, probably in response to the strange energy flow felt in the body. I've seen both boys and girls move closer to Mom during this period, fawning and generally acting like three-year-olds. It must be some kind of reaction to the inner feeling that "this is the time to move away," and these children seldom want to talk about their changing bodies. Other children readily pull away from the parent now, and the parent feels the loss, hurt by the fact that this child is so willing to go.

The crisis is not something that is only experienced by the child, is it? It's a family crisis as well, for as the child is going through his or her own changes, Mom and Dad are going through theirs. Without a helping ritual to get both parent and child through the period naturally, all the energy in the psyche is floating around the house unattended. It makes for quite a bit of tension. This second Jupiter cycle indicates another kind of reaching out—reaching out to the universe as a sexual being.

Age 12-16
First Jupiter Square Jupiter (Second Cycle)
Saturn Opposite Saturn (First Cycle)

At the first square to Jupiter in the second cycle, the reproductive process is well under way, and the young person's body is changing to accommodate the next stage of life. For young women, the body is ready to reproduce. Some of the stress felt is related to the fact that the body is biologically ready to reproduce, but that wonderful body is managed by the brain of a child! Girls fall in love, go steady, play kissy-face games and more, depending on how natal Mars, Venus, and Moon are located in the natal chart.

In some cultures, girls were married at this age, and on farms in the United States some girls still marry now. This is a biologically excellent time to give birth, for the body is supple enough to cope with childbirth, and the girl herself is young enough to essentially grow with her child. Our present-day social structure doesn't allow us to use our bodies at this time, so the physical drives are present, and the young woman can't use them. Or, if she does, she is unprepared emotionally for taking care of a child at this phase of her own development. Parents are understandably upset, and much of the stress between parent and child at this age is related to the girl's budding sexuality. She may not know how to relate to herself, and her parents may not be able to voice the fears they have—and most of the fears will relate in some way to a hope that she doesn't become pregnant.

The young boy begins to experiment with his sex drive now. He's usually uncomfortable with himself because his voice is changing and his body is awkward. He's not sure if he likes girls, or whether he wants to date them. Socially this is a tough period because he may not want to learn to dance or go to parties (unless they are beer parties with the fellas). He doesn't know how to ask a young girl for a date. Learning how to date is a process that is figured out alone, and it is very traumatic. What if she should laugh at him? What if she says no? How does he handle the rejection? What if he likes a girl and she doesn't like him in return? Pulling someone's hair doesn't go over when he's fifteen. All the little-boy techniques of the past don't work anymore and the adult techniques haven't been learned yet.

Some young men and women are so overwhelmed by the changing body, and this new sexual energy, that they avoid dating altogether. We all develop at our own pace, and parents can watch the teenager to see what can be done to help understand this phase of life.

Competition may also be a big issue. This period is extremely competitive in the school system, and some teenagers respond well to competing with their peer group, and others drop out. Fitting into the group is also important—some young people do and some don't. All this relates to the cycle of becoming an adult, for the Saturn opposition may mark a year when the teenager really wrestles with discovering who he or she is within the peer group. The position earned with peers is important, and being allowed to compete is an important phase in this cycle. It helps us learn how we'll do when we test ourselves later in life.

The Saturn opposition to itself brings the relationship with the father and with authority in the outside world into a different focus.

The teenager who rebels during this stage is beginning to test his wings. The pressure is on to leave home, to get away from the nest, to get out on his own. He hasn't realized yet that in order to leave home he has to give up his allowance and he'll have to arrange something about his laundry.

The cycle puts pressure on both parent and teenager, as both are learning to cope with this phase of life. The teenage boy or girl is responding to an inner urge to get out. They want to date and come home when they want to, and the parents object. The father and son often have a go at who runs the house, and who sets up the rules and regulations of the home. If the parents are too lenient, the child doesn't have any boundaries. If the parents are too strict, the child rebels.

One way to work with this cycle is to explain that everyone has a set of rules and regulations. The cycle is saying two things to the child: "Leave home," and because this is a Saturn cycle, it is also saying, "If you want to be an adult you have to assume the responsibilities that go with being one." Saturn represents testing yourself against an authority of some sort in order to learn who you are. If parents are to play the role of authority for the teenager at this time in life, the parents need to give the young person something to fight *against*. If parents are too lenient, the teenager gets worse and worse until the family has to do something, and that something might be rather unpleasant. The cycle of pulling away *must* take place. The parents need to provide the circumstances, or the teenager will have to set them up. Most parents want to be nice to their kids; they want to be friends with their children. Teenagers know they cannot be friends with Mom and Dad because Mom and Dad carry an image in the teenagers' psyche that doesn't include being friends. Parents and children can be friends later on in life, but not at this crucial stage. The cycle needs to be understood in a more traditional framework.

In the teenage counseling situations I've experienced, some of the problems seem to arise from a lack of parental control. The situation goes like this: The kid comes in late, the parents say, "That's okay." The kid smokes cigarettes at home, the parents say, "That's okay." The kid drinks or smokes pot at home, the parents say, "That's okay." Everything the kid does is supported and encouraged by the parents. And suddenly a police officer comes to the door, and the kid has been arrested for stealing a car, and would the parents please come and get him. The kid found his boundaries alright. The most friendly "authority" figure a teenager can come up against is an *understanding* parent, not a *permissive* parent, one who can play the role he or she is forced to play, understanding what the role means in the larger game of life.

For the young woman, the struggle may manifest slightly differently. She needs to rebel against her parents for different reasons. Because the feminine way of rebellion is not always as obvious as a male response, she may rebel sexually. This can manifest in many different ways. She may need to become a more feminine woman than her mother, vying for attention in order to become a woman herself. She may rebel against her father by testing his authority, and starting a relationship he doesn't approve. She may rebel more privately by exploring her own sexuality, hoping to be taken away from home by a knight on a white charger.

In Part 1 it was mentioned that some young people in the "sexual development" phase may be victimized during this stage. Parents are often worried about teenage daughters because the push for freedom may include the possibility of an early pregnancy or unpleasant sexual experiences that could cause emotional scars that last a lifetime. An early pregnancy caused by a loving relationship with a young man is one kind of crisis to handle—for both the parents and the young couple. But that is not the only concern parents have. A physically attractive fifteen-year-old young woman may have no conscious realization that she has a very obvious sexual vibration. This can attract unwelcome advances, and a young woman could, under certain circumstances, be raped by a neighbor, family member, or stranger, and she may not know how to protect herself. Some parents are open about discussing sexual awareness with daughters and some aren't. When parents avoid discussions of this sort, they still worry, for they feel placed in a dilemma: if they warn the child, they may be imposing their own fears on the child unnecessarily; if they don't warn the child, they may feel guilty about leaving the child vulnerable to unpleasant experiences. Some parents don't notice the developing child and refuse to think about this young person's sexuality, while some parents think about it too much.

I have counseled young women who were raped because they walked innocently into a situation that an older woman wouldn't have. I've also counseled young women whose first sexual experience was with a family member—older brother, uncle, etc.—and this happened during the teen years. This is considered incest, but not in the same way that incest is being discussed when it relates to child abuse. The young woman who experienced this unpleasant initiation was often someone who was taught she could "trust" all men. She hadn't been taught how to protect herself should her body become an object of sexual attention from someone with whom she was *familiar*. In the push to become grown-up, which is normal to want to do, she unwittingly became involved in a situation that left deep emotional scars. The most common guilt discussed is that she caused the event to happen, and the next is that she was the only person in her social circle that this ever happened to.

Some say that unpleasant sexual experiences don't happen to boys. That's not true. Most boys don't talk about it, but some have coped with sexual advances from older women in the family or neighborhood. If the young man is emotionally ready for it, society is amused, as illustrated by the movie *The Graduate*. However, when a young man is still in his teens, he can feel immensely threatened by an older woman, and this experience frightens him. In today's culture, we also hear about sexual advances directed toward young men by other men. The object of the advance, according to the people I've talked with, seems to be humiliation. (I'm discussing abuse here, not homosexuality.)

As we become more open about frank discussion of possible human experience, many unpleasant events in life could be alleviated. Perhaps the first Jupiter square and the Saturn opposition illustrate the energy involved in the teen period as life relates to sexuality and freedom. When primitive tribes had sexual initiations, this energy may have been focused for the members of the tribe. Today there is no ritual, many cultures have merged together, and mentally unbalanced people are not diagnosed as such. Some young people are forced to become responsible for themselves sexually in a way that is unfair. Sexual responsibility is a legitimate consideration in life. But it seems unfair to require that teens feel responsible for nasty sexual experience based on either a lack of knowledge or someone else's problem. At the Saturn opposition, the need to become responsible is a valid concern. It is also important that a counselor help young people to differentiate between feeling responsible for the action taken, and that which isn't necessary to assume personally. Too often, a misused boy or girl feels responsible for being innocent or naive. I don't have any answers about how to handle the result of teenage emotional damage, but I do feel that the astrologer should read as much as possible in the field, in order to be better prepared to understand what he or she may hear from a young client.

Age 18-21
Jupiter Opposite Jupiter (Second Cycle)
Last Jupiter Square Jupiter (Second Cycle)
Last Saturn Square Saturn (First Cycle)
First Uranus Square Uranus (First Cycle)

It's hard to tell just how these cycles will overlap. In some charts, they are all active at one time. In others they come along one at a time, making it easier on the young adult who experiences them. It may be that our clients who need crisis counseling need it because the cycles hit all at once and the pressure has become too heavy. We are in need of a ritual passage here, and our society doesn't really give us one. We graduate from high school, or graduate from college, but these are socially prestigious events rather than rituals that have any significance to the psyche as far as the next stage of life is concerned.

The pressure is on to become an adult even more now. As far as Jupiter is concerned (the opposition happening ideally at age 18), physical reproductive development is practically over, and both males and females are ready to reproduce. The sex drive is high unless it has been influenced by inhibitive factors in the home environment. Young adults usually develop serious relationships at this point, or they develop elaborate behavior patterns to hide the fact that they don't want a relationship for some reason. Extremely shy types bury themselves in academia; extremely fearful types have hit-and-run relationships of one kind or another. Usually the basis for this is some problem relating to the whole sexual development process—some discomfort is attached to it.

Many young women marry at this time. Some marry because it is their inclination to marry and raise a family. Some marry because it's the only way to get away from home, or they feel pressured to get out on their own. The Saturn square Saturn may come into play early, and when this happens, relationship problems may arise between the father and daughter, pushing her into a marriage to end the dissension between them. Which it doesn't.

Some young men marry now, again using marriage as a way out of the house. To avoid a critical father, or to start an adult relationship of his own, he strikes off by himself—it's called young love. Sometimes it works and sometimes it doesn't. I've seen cases of very happy marriages that lasted, marriages that were started under this kind of pressure, so who's to say if it's right or wrong? The only thing that the 18-year-old male has to concern himself with is how serious he is in regard to assuming his Saturnian obligations—the reality of paying rent, buying food, paying for expenses that occur when one starts a family. And all this has to be done without Daddy chipping in.

The Saturn square Saturn says that you are now entering the next phase of adulthood. Age 18 was a time when young men were called away to the military service, which could be considered a kind of national ritual that pulled young men away from their mother's apron strings. By serving in the military, men got a chance to experience a number of Saturn influences—such as taking orders, getting up in the morning, having to cope with laundry and making beds, learning to get along with men they didn't like, and having to survive in a group of men without Mom and Dad bailing them out when they ran their mouth and couldn't back it up. The training for survival was also important, for these men were called upon to fight as a team. The importance of being able to defend your tribe (or your land) was an issue even though it wasn't discussed as such. Since mandatory military time has been cancelled, our young men may be losing out on a ritual that is important to survival on an inner level. It was the only ritual we had and maybe it needs to be replaced in some way.

Whether we are male or female, Saturn square Saturn is a part of the developmental process, and part of that development is to become a free-standing member of the tribe. As Joseph Campbell said:

> ...one of the first functions of the puberty rites of primitive societies, and indeed of education everywhere, has always been that of switching the response system of adolescents from dependency to responsibility— no easy transformation to achieve. And with the extension of the period of dependency in our own civilization into the middle or late twenties, the challenge is today more threatening than ever, and our failures are increasingly apparent.[7]

In some ways, the outer-oriented challenges of early adulthood are easier handled by women, for many young women have been taught to play a subordinate role in society—which means they are familiar with coping with unpleasant responsibilities. They are accustomed to doing things they don't enjoy doing, like washing

---

[7]From *Myths to Live By*, by Joseph Campbell. Copyright © 1972 by Joseph Campbell, The Viking Press, New York, 1972, p. 46. Used by permission.

dishes and changing diapers. Handling tasks that "need to be done" can develop an innate sense of responsibility within the "tribe." Taking responsibility is harder for some young men, for there is no ritual to lead them to the next stage in the process of growing up. As Campbell said, the hero journey is one we take alone, and part of the fulfillment of the journey is taking responsibility for each stage of life we encounter, ready or not.

To the young person ready to go on his way during this particular phase of the Saturn cycle, add also the first square of the Uranus cycle. This is the symbol of the first major urge toward individuation, as Uranus symbolizes that process in the natal chart. While Jupiter is saying we should relate on a more conscious level, and Saturn is saying we need to take responsibility for ourselves, Uranus is saying, "Go out there and *be* somebody!" Part of the pressure of pulling away includes pulling away from home and peers. Around age nine, we began to relate to peers—to dress like our age group, to become involved in the fads of our day. Uranus comes along and pushes us to find ourselves for the first time, and we begin to see self-discovery urges manifest.

We suddenly notice that the girl next door is different and we don't know why. She may leave home to pursue a college education in a field in which we never suspected she had any interest. She may become so individualistic that she moves to another city, trying to live with strangers who won't make her feel uncomfortable as she explores her new life. The push to individuation sparks many kinds of reactions.

All three phases of the three cycles have their place, and the crisis occurs when all facets of the personality are not developing as they should for the individual involved. No one can force a young adult to develop—least of all the parents. In order to get the most out of the cycle, Jupiter relating changes and Saturnian increases in personal responsibility will push the young adult so the Uranian process of individuation can start to develop from within.

Part of the trauma of this cycle is a concern with career or education. Sometimes young people know what lifestyle they want to pursue and enroll in college having a particular major in mind. Some people know what kind of work they want to do and direct their energy into a job that brings some gratification. And the rest of us have no idea of what we want to do, so we wallow around a bit, killing time until we get some idea of what our future will be. If we understand that our life's values cannot be fully determined yet, that we have until the Saturn conjunction at the second cycle to find our chosen path, it would give some of us a chance to explore the world differently. Pursuing some kind of education may be more profitable in the long run than becoming a beach bum. Some people don't want to go to college and find themselves by creating a niche in a company that offers immediate rewards in terms of salary increases and personnel evaluations. It doesn't matter whether we handle this cycle perfectly or not; it's important that we understand we are just beginning to explore life.

Age 23-24
Jupiter Conjunct Jupiter (Third Cycle)

We now enter the next crisis phase in our development. The third Jupiter cycle is the official beginning of parenthood and house-holding for many people. The physical body is now developed and we've had a few years to experiment with a sexual role—meaning we've had time to experiment with physical sex, we had an opportunity to decide what we want from sexual activity, we may have already become a parent. During the second cycle (especially from the opposition of Jupiter to itself and through the end of the cycle), most people think they are already grown up. But this growth process includes more than just a body coming into its own and the ensuing sexual experimentation. It is *after* sexual experimentation that one can knowledgeably determine what one wants from sex, or from a sexual relationship.

Most young people think that first love is the be-all and end-all of existence. Those of us who are no longer with our first love know differently. How do you know what you like if you've had no experience? How do you know what you will want in later life? None of us do.

At age 24, we begin the parenting stage in earnest. In other words, we are in the "raising a family" phase of development, and while raising a family, most young adults learn a lot. In this phase biological urges are strong, so many men and women get married during this cycle.

The biological drive will push woman (sometimes almost obsessively) to have a child. Women who are already married become pregnant; some get married and become pregnant immediately; some don't marry and end up having abortions. This is a difficult period for women who are finishing school, for some get pregnant in "spite of themselves," meaning they used a contraceptive, but perhaps absent-mindedly. At any rate, the Jupiter conjunc-

tion signals the possibility of an abortion period that brings on yet
another kind of crisis, for this is a time when women really want to
give birth.

Men want to become fathers, and many of them do. If the more
sensitive male wants children now, and the idea isn't conscious but
remains buried in the psyche, this may signal the hurried marriage
that is formed so parenting can be started. This basis for marriage
may cause conflict later on.

Today's parents are concerned about their offspring starting a
family too early in life. They often think young folk should wait
until they are financially established before having children. They
know how long childraising lasts, and they know how difficult a
marriage can be when the partner isn't suitable, but they can't really
talk to children about it because that might expose various personal
dissatisfactions that are a part of the parents' marriage. So Mom and
Dad may just seem unreasonable in their objections to an early
marriage. On the other hand, this is actually a good cycle to start a
family for it fits in with the growth process that takes place over an
entire life cycle. When we wait too long to have children, we may
wind up combining childrearing with another developmental
cycle. Older parents may find themselves in a different stress
situation as they combine problems that relate to childraising with
interests that pertain to a personal cycle unrelated to the immediate
needs of their child.

The person who elects not to marry or the person who is
essentially homosexual will have to use this energy another way.
Although the norm for the species is to reproduce and raise young
during this cycle, the person who consciously chooses not to will be
better oriented if he or she realizes the cycle exists. This individual is
consciously choosing not to participate in the tribal routine, which
is okay as long as the decision is conscious. It means that there is a
need to establish a life value, a career goal, and a personal
individuality. Usually the more productive individuals in this
group are very career oriented and work extremely hard at some
career goal.

The pitfalls occur when people avoid dealing with the cycle.
These are the people who live blindly, being drawn to unfulfilling
relationships and many disappointments in love. The underlying
cause of cycle avoidance may come to light at the second Saturn
return at age twenty-eight or twenty-nine.

Life for the healthy single person is not just a series of parties
and good times. These individualistic types have a larger stake in

career as far as personal validity is concerned. For example, if you've chosen to be a homosexual, you can't get any "adult points" in your family circle for producing a kid. All the family accolades that would normally come your way for doing anything in regard to producing an heir are not there. The only safe avenue for expression and development is work.

Individuals who have consciously chosen not to marry are often interested in some metaphysical, spiritual, or occult philosophy. Part of the development process is a search for self-knowledge, which also helps direct the life force. Somewhere down the line, the single person will also have to learn something about the concept of parenting, or take the chance of becoming too rigid. Having children accomplishes one thing, if nothing else. It teaches you how to get up at 2 A.M. when you don't want to. It teaches you that there is something more important in life than just yourself, and this develops when a small child is suddenly sick and you have to cope with that experience. That learning experience—consideration for others—is what the single person has to learn alone. If it is not learned, adults become incredibly self-centered. Everything is taken personally, everything is considered as a personal affront, the world revolves totally around these adults. It is difficult for some single people to see how they fit into the scheme of things, for it's hard to see what is outside the sphere of self.

Age 27-30
First Jupiter Square Jupiter (Third Cycle)
Jupiter Opposite Jupiter (Third Cycle)
Saturn Conjunct Saturn (Second Cycle)

This is one of the most critical periods faced by an adult. It is called a crisis because people who don't understand the cycle are really floored by the experience. The average young adult has been told that as soon as he's tall enough he's big enough. Being eighteen is all you need to make it in the adult world. Once you've become an adult, and especially if you have graduated from college, you know it all, and there's nothing more to learn except how to make money. That's not the way life is.

The game that's essentially been run on all of us over these last few centuries is that there isn't any more to life than getting married and raising kids. And maybe going to church to get a dose of God on Sunday. But the internal growth process that is inherent within each of us has not really been explained. Maybe we wouldn't listen anyway.

The first square in this Jupiter cycle brings with it further evaluations about parenthood and adulthood. The relationship between two married people may no longer be fun. No one told us that relationships are work. No one said that you might marry someone who would change, or that you might change. Our movie images show two young people in love—chasing each other down the street—dancing—partying—swimming—driving fast cars—or walking away together into the sunset. Everything is wonderful in the movies. No one writes movies about how to get from Monday to Tuesday on a limited budget with a kid squalling in the background (or even the foreground, which is worse). So both men and women say, "Maybe I oughtta think about this."

If the Saturn conjunction also takes place when the Jupiter square is in, the individual may feel overwhelmed with the energy of the frustration that occurs within this cycle. The Saturn cycle lasts for a year. That's a long time when you have to deal with it every day. Saturn is saying, "Grow up." And Saturn isn't being particularly nice about it. The end result of this feeling is that we all begin to take ourselves rather seriously. We have been playing at being adults up to this point. All through our twenties, society let us play this game, and we really thought we had life figured out. But we didn't.

Actually, what happens is this: We develop as teenagers, and we have a lot of wonderful ideas about how the world ought to be, and how life is going to be for us when we leave home; and in the process of not liking our parents and what they ask of us, we make a deal with ourselves. It basically runs like this: "When I get away from home, I'm going to be a such-and-such." It doesn't matter exactly what the words are, because each person's words will be a little different. And we get out there on our own and we find that such-and-such doesn't work so well. Maybe some of our ideas don't hold water. Often personal ideologies are based on a dislike of what parents have done. "I'll never be like my mother!" says the young woman. But you'll notice that this same young woman is *just* like her mother; maybe the circumstances are a little different, but the underlying behavior is the same.

All the childish games have to go on this Saturn return. If we use a ten-degree applying orb to time this cycle, it gives us a whole year to work with the energy and to learn how to cooperate with it so we can get the most from it. Whether people know astrology or not, the more constructive types automatically fall into step with the cycle. How do we recognize a childish game? We can't get away with it anymore. We pull something at the office, and the boss won't put up with it. If we prove to others that we are untrustworthy or irresponsible, how can we go forward in management? We simply have to make up our mind as to where we want to go as far as work is concerned. If we are doing a good day's work, or handle responsibility well, we will be rewarded for it under this cycle. And if we aren't, we won't. Some of us change careers completely at this time because we suddenly discover what it is that we have always wanted to do. When any career decisions are made during the Saturn return, they're usually made with conviction, and it would be a good idea to listen to that inner voice as long as it isn't angry.

People tend to feel sorry for themselves on this cycle, as it may not be the most pleasant experience. The harder we try to hold on to our outdated ideas, the more they hurt to keep. Authority figures just won't let us have our way now. We are going to grow whether we like it or not. We can survive the cycle without growing very much; I've seen people complain and do nothing but react negatively to everything all the way through it. And when the cycle is over, these folks have missed the boat; they're angry, not any more mature than they were before, and basically they have put themselves in a rut. That's a narrow way to live considering there will be other cycles occurring along the way. This is not a time for postponing the inevitable. This is a key cycle that takes us to the next step of the developmental process.

People do make big changes during this one, and we should not ignore the very important subject of relationships. During the Saturn cycle, we look at our relationships or lack of them. People who are not married or living with someone tend to find a marriage partner or mate. Sometimes it becomes so important to find a mate that we don't pick very well.

For those married couples who still have no children, becoming parents is an issue. Go through the charts of your clients and friends to see how many children have Saturn conjunct the mother's or father's natal Saturn, and you will see a Saturn cycle baby. Many marriages go through hell during this period. If a man married at twenty-four, he probably has a child by the time Saturn returns to its natal place. And he may not like the responsibilities of being married and having to care for a child. Care for a child? Yes, the responsibility of being concerned about a child, whether you actually change the diapers or not.

If the marriage survives the Saturn cycle, remember that she is probably younger than he is, and in a few years she will also go through a Saturn return. And she will then evaluate whether or not she wants this marriage. Influencing her decision may be a Jupiter opposite Jupiter, and the word thirty. When the female goes through the Saturn return she changes a great deal. The male usually becomes more serious about his career and really makes long-range plans to attain a goal. The female, on the other hand, not only makes decisions about her career, but also starts thinking about herself as a person.

During her twenties, the young woman is easily molded. If she loves some guy and he doesn't want her to do certain things—like study astrology—she won't. After the first Saturn return, the chances are she will study whether he likes it or not. She becomes much stronger, more forceful, less willing to deal with the okey-doke stuff that can be dished out to women by some men. She no longer takes it. She talks back. He's unhappy. This may end the relationship, for the man she's married to may be completely unprepared for the change in her attitude. Well, she's preparing for womanhood, and she can't be in control of her personality, or develop it, if she is doomed to play an anima role.

How do single people handle the Saturn return? The same way the married people do, except the circumstances are different. The issue here is about maturation, and the single person becomes more motivated as far as career is concerned, usually taking this time to make great strides. As far as personal life is concerned, changes will take place there as well, for we become more serious about ourselves. The issue of sex is a big one; meaningful sexual relationships are becoming more important than experimental sex. You can only experiment for so long before you become jaded, and at the Saturn return, there is a good chance that you won't take part in relationships that end up being chalked off to another learning experience. Commitments become important. Women find they want some kind of commitment, even if they are not looking for marriage. Gay couples tend to pair up now, and even move away from the more social gay community in order to build a life structure that has more meaning.

The crisis connected with a Saturn cycle is enough of a trauma to go through without ending a relationship that has already begun. If a bad relationship needs to end now, it will. But it can also be talked out. No woman wants to see a man go through his Saturn cycle; he's too serious, he doesn't want to have fun, he wants to work. He may be considering a totally new career and this makes his mate nervous. When a man is going through a major career trauma he may become totally disinterested in sex. This can make his partner feel unwanted and very insecure.

The woman going through this cycle is now becoming a person. This can be a total shock to her partner, who never saw this side of her before. She may be concerned with her own career, and this may threaten him. She may want to establish a family now. Or she may want to do both. A number of women in New York City had children on the Saturn return, and went back to work, spending their entire salary on childcare. Career was important to them, but so was having a family. In more tribal societies it was not uncommon for women to take care of a number of other women's babies; it is only recently that we programmed the need for mothers to be totally in charge of offspring at all times. Many new-age mothers are giving their children into a tribal group, and prefer to spend more time working with the child's mind than with the diapers.

Women also start to talk like they never have before during this cycle. A woman may speak with too much venom because she's not used to expressing herself. This is a period for talk, and in partnerships the person who cares enough to listen to her as she goes through this phase of maturation will listen. If she is to grow from an anima image into a matriarch or a wise woman someday, she has to learn how to express herself as a person. Personal relationships are the most difficult places to do this. Have you ever seen the competent woman in an office work efficiently all day, relate to fellow employees as a grown-up, witty individual, and then seen her act like a dumb-dumb around her husband? I have. She hasn't allowed him to join her as her personality has developed, and she is creating a split that will eventually separate them because she's closing him out of her development.

In order to counsel this cycle, I've found that just explaining what is in store for the individual is really enough. I usually talk about the bad side first and then explain all the wonderful things that can come from using the energy constructively. I don't know what the counseling of the future will be, for people are changing. The people I counseled in New York were go-getters. Most young people who come to the city are looking for something, and the process of individuation is a part of that. So they were quite receptive to the idea of growing up.

I've recently met people in their late twenties who are absolutely dynamic while going through the Saturn return, and it's exciting to talk with them. However, there are a number of young people who may have trouble facing the decisions involved with this cycle. Gail Sheehy makes some interesting observations about this period in *Pathfinders*, and uses the term "postponer" to describe the individual who avoids confronting becoming responsible.

Sheehy searched out people of all ages who had survived crisis, calling them "pathfinders" because they had faced the crisis of a passage of initiation in life, and as a result of this passage, had become more mature people. But she notes that new problems are confronting young people who are striving for a place in today's world. A major issue for women is children; many are avoiding having them altogether in favor of developing a career. Others just postpone having to make the decision at all. Some women she interviewed were intensely planning careers five to ten years ahead of time—while still in their twenties! Children and career can be combined, but many young women don't see it that way. Men were concerned with work in a different way: the idea of working as hard as their fathers did, at the sacrifice of what they called emotional self-development, has become a new issue. As Sheehy notes,

> The irony is that while the bright young women are indoctrinated into Old-Boy timing, the pacesetting men of our society recently have begun to question, *Why should I work so hard? What else am I missing in life?*[8]

> The educated new young man in my studies is decidely a postponer. The centerpiece in his game plan is to remain unattached, at least until he is 30, and to keep his career line tentative. Here, in particular, he is breaking new ground. The majority of his father's generation chose as their life pattern to launch all three aspects—career, marriage, and family—in their early twenties.[9]

These are the children of the professionals who had no time to spend with their kids. Many of today's young people feel that parents owe them time, owe them something they didn't get, but they too aren't prepared to give a lot, either to family or peer relationships.

Sheehy brings up several issues that could be considered in terms of counseling cycles. Young women going through the Saturn return in future years may need specific counseling in regard to combining career goals and parenting, as these issues relate to

---

[8]See *Pathfinders*, Gail Sheehy, Bantam Books, New York, 1982, p. 159.

[9]See *Pathfinders*, Gail Sheehy, Bantam Books, New York, 1982, p. 146.

natural cycles. The young men Sheehy interviewed seem to be more involved in postponing activities formerly thought to be important in our society. In previous generations, young men combined career, marriage and parenting in their early twenties. Many young men today want to avoid making career decisions or marriage plans. As the Saturn conjunction approaches, the inner drives of the developing individual may push to be heard.

After interviewing thousands of people using the same questionnaires, including questions about feelings of well-being, Sheehy reports that the postponing generation wants to make no decisions at all. Childhood expectancies were formed while living high off the hog, and present day financial conditions imply that these same people will have trouble buying a house, or doing what their parents did. Postponing life creates problems all around, as the young men are concentrating on being free and open, while the educated young woman may be concentrating on career. Personal freedom and the quest for personal satisfactions may set up new problems, because the family structure may become even weaker.[10] Eventual financial struggles caused by needing a two-income relationship will ultimately bring about different emotional problems that will need to be counseled. It will be interesting to watch how this manifests later in the cyclic pattern.

Age 31-33
Last Jupiter Square Jupiter (Third Cycle)

This crisis may be very small compared to what we've just been through. The third Jupiter cycle is coming to a close. Events that happened at the Jupiter opposition (about age thirty) need to be clarified now. Choices and perspectives are changing. For the women who had children in their early twenties, this Jupiter square will bring up, briefly at least, the concept of a change coming—they may no longer be needed all day to take care of the children. What will they do now? This is a time for career development for some women.

For men, it's a busy time if the Saturn cycle was handled well. They may be so immersed in work, they need to be reminded they have a relationship. The concept of relating—to keep personal relationships from stagnating into empty role-playing—may be the issue at hand under this Jupiter emphasis and this involves both single and married people.

---

[10]See *Pathfinders*, Gail Sheehy, Bantam Books, New York, 1982, pp. 145-163.

Age 35-36
Jupiter Conjunct Jupiter (Fourth Cycle)
First Saturn Square Saturn (Second Cycle)
Maybe Neptune Square Neptune (First Cycle)
Maybe Pluto Square Pluto (First Cycle)

This Jupiter conjunction starts the fourth Jupiter cycle. It's going to add something to your concept of relating, isn't it? You've got your body, your sexuality, your kids. The next stage of life involves sharing. Up until this point, each of us has been trying to establish a personality. The rhetoric may go something like this: "I am a Mommy [or a daddy]. I am a successful career person. I love someone. I have a child that I love. I [may] own a house that I bought. I have a mate." But that's not all there is to life—for the sharing concept is coming into play. In order to develop fully, we have to learn to share our ideas, time, space, to really let another person in. We have to learn to share our kids, and in this process we need to learn how to let them go. If the Jupiter return at age thirty-six relates to becoming parents at age twenty-four, then your children are now entering the stage of puberty. Which means that many people have a teenage child who is in the process of becoming a man or a woman. It's time for the parent to teach these children about life. It's time to consider letting them go. It's time to begin to expand consciousness to the needs of the neighborhood in which we live. The adult perspective will be growing into a different phase over the next twelve years. For those who work, it's time to begin to teach others how to do your job. It's time to stop doing everything alone and to begin to allow others to share in the work load.

At this Jupiter return, most men are completely immersed in career. The wife and kids are a side issue. Life is seen in terms of the deals one can make, the moves one can handle, the houses one can buy. It's a pomp and circumstance period. Men are going so strong at this age, they feel sure they'll own the business at forty. No one can stop them. They don't look around to see how they're doing; they think nothing can stand in their way.

Meanwhile, back home, if his wife is his age, he has no idea of what's going on with her. The woman in her mid-thirties has just discovered that she must let go of her children. The phase of being a mother-constantly-in-demand is wearing thin. She doesn't know what to do with her life. Her husband isn't paying attention to her, and she may be feeling unattractive. Her youth is going, and, after all, the American dream is the twenty-year-old surfing on the California beaches with a soft-drink in her hand. So she may find another man who makes her feel attractive and desirable again. No one may know she has a husband, a family and a lover. However, her counselor may have to help her cope with the stress of a situation of this nature. Some women feel they should divorce the husband and marry the lover. This may not be a good idea; it should be carefully thought out before taking any action, for the lover may only be needed until she feels her sense of self-worth returning. He may not be the companion she wants for a long-term relationship.

Some women divorce on this cycle. The husband is usually irate because divorces don't look good on his company record. He needs to have the perfect wife on his arm whenever he needs the perfect wife, and he hasn't planned on her upsetting the applecart. When he comes down off the high horse of success, he may realize that he has ignored his wife beyond any reasonable doubt—and may begin to value his relationship again. And he, too, may be playing around. If he's on the way up, his office is full of young women who find powerful men fascinating, and some young women want to have an affair but don't want to wash the dirty socks. The point of all this is: does your sense of self-worth come from inside yourself or outside? If your value is determined only by those who find you attractive, your older years may be pretty uncomfortable.

At age thirty-five or so, the first square from Saturn (second cycle) appears. This involves some replanning of the career goal that was launched at the Saturn conjunction. Perhaps some adjustment that relates to what we just discussed needs to be made. Perhaps, in the midst of a career struggle, we need to take the time to work our relationship onto another plane. Once the children are old enough to demand less care, the parents may need to re-establish the relating stuff that brought them together in the first place. During the first few years of a child's life, the child is so demanding, so full of need, that there is little time for a personal relationship. Husbands and wives forget why they got married. This is a time to get to know each other again.

To digress a minute, this Jupiter cycle forms the basis of the next twelve years of growth. When married people cater totally to the needs of children, dinner is controlled by children's conversation, the husband comes home from work to hear about what little Johnny did wrong, the dinner table is full of squabbling, and adults have no time to talk. A crying baby needs attention, but a whining twelve-year-old doesn't. What mothers don't understand is that they block the noise of their children, but the husband doesn't. Suddenly he doesn't want to go home, because there is no peace there. The couple doesn't talk anymore, many couples go for years without doing anything social that doesn't include the children, and the relationship deteriorates into a mythic mother/father image. You will hear these people even referring to each other as "Mother" and "Father." When the children leave the nest, they will either leave behind two unified people or two empty shells, and the choice is ours to make.

If Neptune is also coming into a square to itself, we add to our confusion the nebulous energy of that planet; it seeps into our beds and our dreams, and eventually into our waking consciousness, to ask us how we like our dream. If Neptune symbolizes our concept of inspiration, our dreams, and wishes, then the square will bring questions to mind regarding our dream goals. The gossamer veil is lifted from our lovely idea and we find something not as pretty as our illusion. If we have been pursuing a dream, if we began to follow a dream that was only a faint glimmer in our mind's eye when we were in our teens and early twenties, what has happened? The dreamer wakes up and realizes that she is in the middle of a house full of dirty dishes and screaming kids. Whatever was she reaching for? And he comes home to find a disheveled wife, the house a mess, dinner not done, with a bunch of screaming kids waiting for him to get through the door, and he wonders what kind of a life he is pursuing and for what.

Rather than discussing the shattered images and broken dreams, both husband and wife have been known to take to drinking. When she can't stand it anymore, there is always the 4 P.M. martini. And when he can't stand coming home at night, he may have a martini on the train or in a bar near the office, only coming home for another one before dinner. The noise gets drowned out that way. When this happens, the Neptune energy may be keeping you from facing what needs to become conscious now. This may be a bit out of context, but Richard Bandler said in a discussion about neurolinguistic programming that people usually see what they have set themselves up to see. While operating out of our own internal world, we are trying to find out what matches it.

> One of the best ways to have lots of disappointment in your life is to construct an image of how you would like things to be, and then try to make everything that way. You will feel disappointed as long as the world doesn't match your picture. That is one of the best ways to keep yourself in a constant state of disappointment, because you are never going to get the world to match your picture.[11]

---

[11]See *Frogs into Princes, Neuro Linguistic Programming*, Richard Bandler and John Grinder, Real People Press, Moab, Utah, 1979, p. 46.

The Neptune crisis brings on a need for change. Old dreams dissolve to make way for a new reality. The new reality doesn't have to happen to you, it can be created by you, but you have to want to see who you are and where you are going in order to change. Closing off, and trying to obliterate what is happening won't do it for you in the long run.

And if the Pluto square Pluto is in orb during this age, what else do you think will happen? Pluto is an unseating influence. It, too, is a nebulous transit. At least Saturn is obvious—you know what you're learning. But Pluto doesn't work that way. You get vague feelings that something isn't right. If Pluto symbolizes the unconscious motivation of your generation, and your response to those drives is basically unconscious, then you're coping with an unseen enemy. If you don't know about the cycle, it can work very slowly at undermining self-confidence.

Considering the new Jupiter cycle along with the Saturn square, women are unsure of who they are and men are skating along the brink, skating along on ice they hope will hold them up, for the chances are they are skimming. If we stop to look inside what do we see? Who wants to look? Maybe we'll see that deep down within ourselves there are all these ugly things just waiting to rear their ugly heads. Maybe we'll see that we are still selfish, greedy, competitive, fearful, dependent, jealous, possessive and even a bit self-destructive. Who wants to look at that? And to top it off, we are in our middle-thirties, life is almost half over and we are still not grown up. No one can help us out of this bottleneck except ourselves.

Age 37-42
First Jupiter Square Jupiter (Fourth Cycle)
Jupiter Opposite Jupiter (Fourth Cycle)
Uranus Opposite Uranus (First Cycle)
Maybe Neptune Square Neptune (First Cycle)
Maybe Pluto Square Pluto (First Cycle)

This is probably the most stressful period that we will ever experience in terms of life cycles. People are beginning to joke about midlife crisis, but it really isn't a joke. As you know, we tend to treat what we find difficult with humor, for if we don't laugh we might cry.

One of the best descriptions of midlife crisis has been written by Gail Sheehy in her now famous *Passages*.[12] She certainly gave me some insight into my own midlife passage—she really hit the nail on the head. When I was much younger, I used to counsel midlife crisis, based on what I had heard from my teachers or from astrologers who lectured at astrological conferences. The counseling seemed to help clients through this trying time. They came back for more, which is a sure sign to an astrologer that the compliment made after the session wasn't just a courtesy. But when I experienced midlife crisis myself, I couldn't imagine how I had been able to be of any help at all! No matter how much preparation is made for this event, it turns out differently than you expect. It wasn't until I read, and reread, *Passages* that I began to feel better, and I earnestly recommend that anyone wishing to counsel cycles explore this book.

At midlife crisis we feel that we have reached the apex in life. We need to reassess our lifestyle to see where we've been and where we are going. We need to re-examine the goals we've set for ourselves perhaps for the first time since we made them many years ago. Sheehy talks about discovering that we have only so much time to find our own *truth*. Most people feel that time is running out. We begin to wonder if we can accomplish it all before it's too late—too late for what? Too late because we are going to die someday, that's what. The aging process has set in. How awful! Look at your chin— or your knees. Both men and women begin to sag a bit at the edges. Career go-getters wonder if they will ever make it, and women who have spent their lives doting on children wonder if they will be able to fill their days when the children are gone from home forever.

I mentioned that I had a difficult time with the cycle. I really thought I had prepared for it, for I know all the dates and the time periods, and had some general understanding of what would occur. I knew I had to bend and change, and I was ready to change. But I wasn't ready for the changes that actually occurred—I was ready for others. Hopefully that statement will help someone else planning to "ease on down the road" when this cycle takes place. The information Sheehy presents ties in beautifully with our astrological symbolism. If one cycle takes place at a time, we can work our way through the crises more easily than when all the cycles are active at once. It's not that this cycle is difficult to survive; it's that this is a rough one to handle because we may not be prepared for the internal changes that take place.

[12]See *Passages,* Gail Sheehy, Bantam Books, New York, 1976.

The most important thing to remember is that Jupiter affects you for two months and Uranus will affect you for two years. The energy creates a situation that can provide some trying times, as there is a tendency to want to leave everything you've known and start all over. It won't work—because you have to deal with the death aspect of the cycle, which we shall discuss later.

First let's look at Jupiter. The first Jupiter square in the fourth cycle indicates an adjustment that needs to be made regarding the last Jupiter conjunction. If you aren't adding anyone to your life, if you are not sharing, you'll be made aware that you are not up to par. Somehow you have to become more open, and it's important to allow others into your life. Retreating into yourself is not what this cycle wants, yet this may be exactly what you want to do because of the other cycles that may be present. The more you fight opening up, the more you may be forced to deal with outside energies because of external circumstances. You may end up being very grouchy and unsociable, which usually indicates that something doesn't want to change. However, to start this new phase (the second major phase) of your life, you have to open up somehow.

When the Jupiter opposition takes place later in midlife, you will know whether or not your relationship decision was a good one—either your relationships with others will become closer or they won't. You may find yourself talking with your mate more than you did before, and you may be talking about different subjects. You may find that you've become more involved in family responsibilities (*i.e.,* relatives or children) than you were before. You may find that your relationship to either your mother or father is changing. Or you may discover that you are cementing close relationships with friends who have become much more important to you—and you are doing this in a way you were unable to in the past.

If you lose a parent during this period, you may feel a different kind of aloneness than people who lost parents in their teens or twenties. If your parents lived to a ripe old age, no matter what moves you made in your relationships or career, there was some kind of anchor in your psyche—whether you liked your parents or not—that kept you attached to some umbilical cord somewhere. When you lose your parents during this cycle, that tie is broken, and you *finally* realize that you are completely alone in this world; this awareness can be a bit depressing. Once you lose your mother, you "can't go home again," as they say, and when your dad is gone, you can't discuss any of your plans to see if he supports or disapproves of them. The loss of a parent will add to the burden—and also brings up another phase of the death experience.

Uranus opposing itself says that you must make something of your life; maybe you should leave your career, marriage, neighborhood, and start something new. It's not a bad idea if you think it out carefully first. Uranus indicates that it is time to change. The last major push you had from this energy was when you left home at the end of school. This is a push to a new phase of development. It is a time for change, but it doesn't mean that you have to end a relationship or leave a job. It means that you need to view your life differently.

As far as relationships are concerned, for those with families it might be a good idea to discuss the energy and the inclinations with your partner. Children will be leaving home soon. This is an opportunity for couples to get to know each other all over again, and some changes will need to be made to take the relationship to its next level of possibility. She is no longer the "sweet little anima figure" and he is no longer the "big hero on the white charger." They have both sagged a bit; they have both developed a completely different personality than they had when they met. And it may be time to share those differences in an exciting new way.

In relationships where there are no children, in order to keep the relationship alive it must change. Some differences in attitude need to be worked out, and the communication level probably should change. As men and women age, they become more alike, so it's harder to maintain the "his" and "her" role. Two people who grow old together come full circle in both the personality and the sexuality department. For example, when a woman is young, she needs a lot of foreplay to become sexually aroused. The male doesn't. Some of the sexual problems that young couples experience are based on the fact that the male ejaculates before the woman has been satisfied. As the aging process continues, the woman becomes more easily aroused, and when she is through with menopause, she still has a strong sex drive. The male now needs more foreplay, however. Couples can learn different ways of making love—if they are open to that—and the sex roles may change a lot. If the couple is not open, and will not allow for these physical changes to take place, a lot of tension starts to build up now because neither is comfortable talking about the changes taking place but both of them *notice* the changes.

Part of the fear of growing older is the fear of losing one's sex drive. It's very amusing, but do you know what we do? When we were younger, we thought that our parents never made love. In all the years of counseling I've done, most young people think that their parents never "made it," and they think that the parents were so cold that most children consider themselves to be an "immaculate conception." However, the truth of the matter is that most parents have quite a sex life, but the kids don't know about it—nor should they. All kids think that old people (anyone over thirty!) don't do "it" anymore. I said all this to get to my point. We *still* (when we ourselves are adults) think that if *we* get older *we* won't have a sex life because our parents didn't! Now isn't that a funny idea? Half of our midlife concern about our failing sexuality is probably based on a memory that says, "Mom and Dad are too old to do 'it' anymore." Ridiculous! We don't need to worry about sex, for it can become more fun and more fulfilling as we get older, for we are not doing "it" for the same reasons we did it at age twenty-one.

So—back to the subject at hand—your relationship will change. It will need to alter so that the two of you can grow, the two of you can develop your sense of self, and you can both go through whatever it is that you need to go through to process your own particular individuation experience. This cycle is the beginning of it all! Kids are old enough to give parents free time. If you didn't have kids, you are now old enough to get past your own selfish stuff to see what living is all about.

For most people, a marriage or other lasting relationship is formed on a basic anima/animus relationship. Jung says in *The Development of Personality* that in order for both partners to grow, they have to cope with some kind of shock since insights do not come easily to any of us![13] He discusses how a man, in the career process, breathes his own life into things and risks being *overgrown* with the things he has created, while his wife is *overtaken* with her children. All that has been created up until this point in life has essentially taken on a life of its own, and now the middle years signify a need to let go of that and start something new. What's new? The fact that in the very period of life when everything seems to be going well, the second half of life begins. It is a tremendous changeover—suddenly the climb *up* the moutain is beginning to turn into the walk down. Jung says that this is a time when we must discover our real motivations. He also says that this will only be

---

[13] See *The Development of Personality*, C. G. Jung, translated by R. F. C. Hull, Bollingen Series XX, Pantheon Books, New York, 1954, p. 193.

done the hard way. The path of individuation—the development of personality—is not an easy one. And it is a path that involves assuming responsibility for yourself. This is why it's so important for partners to share in the change during midlife crisis, for each must become an individual—no longer can one act out the anima/animus role for the other, for if they do, the development of personality cannot take place.

Most people who write about midlife crisis say that if you are successful by the time you're forty, it doesn't make you happy, and if you are not successful by the time you're forty, you're not happy either! People who work too hard are often brought down the hardest by midlife crisis, for something comes along and knocks them off their feet—either a major illness or something happens that is job related. Whatever happens, these people have to stop short and take a look at what's going on in their lives. People who are not strongly career motivated, who realize that age isn't so threatening after all, seem to change into people who can relax more. They take crises in their stride, and can find something else to do. Either type of personality needs counseling, however, for the aim of any counseling at this stage would be to avoid slipping into the "through at fifty" syndrome.

With Neptune looming on the horizon for its first square, many hopes are shattered during this period. Whatever the individual's dream or goal, whatever the source of inspiration, something will dissolve now, and some phase of life will have to be sorted out. With the pressure from Jupiter and Uranus, and with the disappointments brought to light via the Neptune square, the midlife crisis person may become despondent and depressed. The suicide rate (at its prime age forty-one, until a few years ago) reflects some of this hopelessness. A person who has no one to talk with about personal troubles may be forced over the edge by disillusionment. These suicides may be linked to personal depression, the failure of a career, a marriage breakup, or all of the above.

Pluto could be squaring itself during this time as well, but this will depend on the year of birth. Pluto's energy will bring additional crisis. It is said to symbolize the unconscious motivation of a generation, and if natal Pluto is tied to the personal planets in the birth chart, this becomes an important factor—the motivation for change is now personal, and comes from the unconscious depths of the personality. Plutonic energy causes feelings of "being out of control" and the owner of the aspect may feel really alone. Imagine how you would feel if all this energy were manifesting at the same time, and you have just become aware of your mortality—or immortality.

Just for fun, let's thicken the plot, and add Pluto's energy. Think of the crisis that could take place if you followed your Uranus energy and changed careers, and then Pluto square Pluto comes into orb. Between the Pluto square and the Neptune square, you might put yourself into the following dilemma: You've left your old job. You're involved in something new and untried. Your sense of values, and more importantly, of being valued, comes from the praise and position you held in your previous job. No one knows you in your new business venture. Neptune dissolves some nice belief systems that you once held, and Pluto brings in a fear of loss and a fear of being out of control. This loss of control might actually be happening in business because you are just starting something new and have yet to become familiar with it. All your feelings of self-worth or personal worthiness are being tested. You may value yourself, but in these new circumstances no one outside of yourself is giving you any feedback. If you have a strong marriage and a mate who is supportive at this time, you can pull through without too many problems, especially if you are conscious enough to be able to discuss this with your mate. But what if your mate is busy? Or what if you've just left an old relationship? Where does your nurturing come from? How long can you hold out without succumbing to a feeling of failure?

Sheehy talks about the fear of death, and the new consciousness of death that emerges during midlife crisis. It's not that we have been previously unaware of death, but this is something that is just becoming real to us. We are in the second half of life now, and we are on the way down the mountain. We might die any minute; some of our friends are dying right now. We may experience a life-threatening illness which brings us very close to the concept of our own death. No matter how the death concept gets activated, it brings to life a fear of dying, a concern about death, even a preoccupation with death. Once the cycle passes and we feel more comfortable with the idea of "yes, we will not get out of this life alive," we settle in to become much more comfortable with it.

At midlife, the fear of death, or an abrupt awareness of death may be caused by a sudden realization that life is passing us by. All at once we realize that life is at the halfway mark. People in their twenties and thirties are trying so hard to accomplish something in the future that they don't consider their own death—they are too involved in *being*. The consciousness that appears at midlife crisis may be related in some way to the Jupiter cycle, causing us to enlarge our scope, broaden our vision, to think of something other than self alone. Up to this point, much of our "we" conversation has been a kind of lip service. Now we have another role to play. Yes, we are alone. Yes, we can never really share our inner "self" with anyone. But we are a part of a collective group, and a collective consciousness that far surpasses what we thought it could.

If midlife crisis is so bad, why not just sleep until it's over? Life doesn't work that way. In the maturation process, if the second half of life is to be lived to its capacity, then we have to get on with the changes at hand. Midlife crisis is essentially a rebirth. The trauma of any birth is not pleasant, but then change isn't easy. What has to change? Relationship attitudes and concepts, the value of the personality, one's goals and visions of the future, and one's connections with the generation into which one is born. Slowly over the next few years, after this crisis is over, the maturing person realizes a change in role. As the Hindus would say, the householder is beginning to let go, and the free person is beginning to emerge from the cocoon.

Age 43-45
Last Jupiter Square Jupiter (Fourth Cycle)
Saturn Opposite Saturn (Second Cycle)
Maybe Pluto Square Pluto (First Cycle)

The push for change isn't over yet. For several months, under the Jupiter square Jupiter, we again have to analyze how we're doing in the fourth Jupiter phase of relating. Are we supportive to our children? Are we beginning to teach them or anyone else? Are we sharing what we know with anyone? If no changes have been made in our personal relationships, some event will occur to make us aware of how we missed the mark. The cycle should not promote fear but rather an openness to change. If we have missed the mark, events that occur will put us back on course, if we pay attention. It's better to grow now, for it we don't, we'll bring our lacks into the next Jupiter cycle.

The Saturn opposition indicates that the first half of the second cycle is coming to an end. If our decisions at the conjunction (age twenty-eight or so) were good for us, the opposition will show the culmination of a period of growth which should lead to some recognition of our worth. If we did not make a good decision at the conjunction, the opposition will show that too. We now begin to work with the last half of the cycle, and some people settle for middle-management and the status quo as far as career is concerned. Others begin to plan for new interests. The strongly motivated career person will adjust career goals in some way, either reaping benefits or realizing that a change of direction is needed. Women may experience a new career drive because this is the first time the Saturn energy can be channeled in that direction; earlier, it may have been channeled toward raising children.

We're not on the way up anymore; we are now in a phase of expressing who we are and sharing what we have learned. By this phase of the Saturn cycle we should have something to offer. Many people join career-related groups and give time, sharing expertise gained over the years. Some people, who have not been strongly career motivated, may join community organizations or try to help the neighborhood, the city, or the state. Some become involved in political activities if the larger concept of the well-being of the country becomes an important issue for them.

This is a time to think about giving back what you have become. For some this is a trying time, if they don't know who they have become. If the self-image is distorted, this doesn't signify an unhealthy person, but rather someone who has been so busy in the process of *becoming* that he or she has not taken the time to see the person who has emerged. Outsiders may draw you up short on this cycle, for you may be treated in a way you don't expect to be treated, or you may be given a position in the community, in your field, or in a new social group. You may feel uncomfortable about this until you realize people are treating you differently than you see yourself. Saturn transits always allow for a change in perspective, and the crystallization—or becoming conscious—of who you have become is needed. This is not an ego-bending discussion I'm having here. It has nothing to do with ego. It has to do with recognizing your worth and the image you create in your community, whether you are trying to or not. If someone, for instance, starts to sincerely study law, first there is the cycle of being the student, then you get your degree, then you start to practice, but you know you are still wet behind the ears. You look up to people in the field who are older and more experienced, who command your respect. You may even strive toward being as good a lawyer as so-and-so. You work hard for a number of years, and you come to this Saturn opposition, and begin to realize that there are new people in the profession, who come along and say that they admire *your* work, *your* expertise, the way *you* handle a case. Suddenly what *you* say and what *you* do become important, and you realize that you are setting an example for others. And this is something you may not have set out to do at all. You may know inside yourself that you still have a great deal to learn, you've just broadened your vision, and within your consciousness is a whole new scope of what you want to do with your future, and how you will think in the future. So you're still learning. But you are also in a position to be a teacher, and you can teach best what you've left behind you while still going forward to learn what it is that you want to add to yourself.

Not all of us are going to become great lawyers. But in any profession, community, or family, we have this same role to play on some level. In the family, we may become aware that we are in training for the position of "head of the tribe" even though we may not want the position. Each phase of life brings on a new role to play.

If Pluto is squaring itself during this period, then the unsettling conditions symbolized by Pluto will also push us in another direction. A larger process is at stake here, for your life goals, as they fit into your community, will be an issue. If Pluto symbolizes the unconscious motivation of a generation, the values of your generation relate to you personally, because you are either a part of the value system or you disagree with it. In either case you play a role that relates to the generation to which you were born. If Pluto is tied to the personal planets in your natal chart, the square will be even more significant, for the changing values of your generation will affect you in a personal sense.

One of the effects of the Pluto change may express as a subtle loss of goal orientation. You may find yourself in a stressful situation if you feel out of control on some inner level. This may manifest as not being sure of where you are going, and it may be best to learn how to "tread water" until the changing self emerges from the depths of the Pluto energy. A new goal is in the process of manifestation, and you may have no idea what that goal or purpose is yet. It will definitely involve a rebuilding within yourself of some characteristic or purpose that is built on the ashes of the old one—a new emergence of personality, a new emergence of energy.

It's interesting to consider that midlife crisis is essentially a rebirth—being born again into the second stage of life. In our middle forties we don't respond with the same openness of the three-year-old reaching out to a new universe, do we? Some of our innocence and naivete is gone, but we have more to offer for we have a more developed mind.

Age 46-50
Jupiter Conjunct Jupiter (Fifth Cycle)
Last Saturn Square Saturn (Second Cycle)

For many people midlife crisis happens with the Saturn and Uranus oppositions. For others it continues for a longer period. Whatever your belief, we now start the fifth Jupiter cycle and this should push us into the realm of the grandparent, whether it be physical or mental grandparenting. For parents, it's important to begin to let go of the children, to let them stand on their own two feet, so you can be freed. This is unpleasant for some parents, as they find the confrontation difficult. Children may accuse parents of not caring because parents are no longer totally available—at the child's convenience, of course. Parents say, "Of course I'm still here. Here's some money." When we don't know what to do in order to get rid of our children, it may be helpful to get some lessons from the animals who still know they are animals. When the maturing puppy or kitten returns to mother still looking to nurse, essentially able to take care of itself, the mother is nice for a few moments and then she gives the young one a cuff. Not too hard. If the youngster still returns, she cuffs a bit harder until the message is received. Maybe we ought to give this a try.

The problems we have in releasing our children are twofold. Either we feel guilty about doing it because we really have had enough of childraising and can't admit it, or we can't let go of the children because we haven't discovered anything to replace them with. If we observed our cycles in the strictest sense, and if we raised a family according to the natural cyclic energy, children will be about twenty-four years old when we experience this cycle. Which means the child is now ready to produce children. Therefore the grandparent role. We are free to step away, even if our own children have decided not to become parents themselves.

The grandparent cycle means that we can give our children time in limited amounts. We give up the parenting role; the new young parent becomes the householder, and the new young parent takes care of his or her children, and also takes care of the needs of his parents. By this time, we should be considering the next Jupiter cycle—of letting our children (or other young people) begin to help us. We all need to learn how to accept help and care at this juncture of our lives. If we can allow ourselves to accept from others, we are really freeing something within ourselves so we can take part in the next process of our growth—that of opening up spiritually.

How does this cycle work if we never married, or if we never had children? Whether or not you are a parent, the grandparenting stage still comes into play. The role you play in life is changing, and since you don't need to get away from your family, it provides a different set of circumstances with which to work. You have to leave something behind—I have no idea of what the something is, but you will when it is appropriate. Rigidity is a key word, for something in your life plan needs to change in order to keep you from becoming a totally rigid personality.

The philosophical side of yourself is ready for developing and you are just starting the cycle. You need to be ready to share, to allow others to help you, to feel that your physical independence is not a matter of pride. Your body is changing and you need to learn how to use it differently. The ability to distance yourself from emotional situations, to learn to see the bird's-eye-view of life, to develop a different perspective, is on your agenda.[14] If you work, your new insights will be incorporated there as well. As you think, you will notice your perceptions change.

Single people often have a better chance at raising consciousness because they literally have the time to do it. No one has more control over their lives than someone who lives alone or who has decided not to have children. The demands are usually greater as well, for the single person has more time to look inside—to see developments in life—both physical and spiritual. And the single person can never use a child as a cop-out, saying, "Well, at least my kid got a college education." Because there isn't any kid.

The last square of Saturn to itself brings the career cycle to a close for some people. At the beginning of the second Saturn return (age twenty-eight) we vowed to take ourselves seriously, to build a

---

[14]To show an example of the change in perspective, when I was working for a company that was involved in a merger I was also involuntarily involved in a power struggle among some of our company's executives. I was very hurt after being unnecessarily attacked, and was ready to leave the company in anger. One such mature lady sat me down and said, "Betty, wait. You're being paid a good salary and have a good position because someone here thinks you should be in the position you have. Wait." And of course she was right as the problem cleared itself up in a short time. A difference in perspective between an older more mature lady executive, and a young hothead.

career and a life for ourselves. We decided to become realists. We built a family or a career that would structure the next twenty-eight years of our life. Twenty-one years later, we now look to see how we've done and we look to see how much time we have left in our chosen lifestyle.

For men, this period marks some changes in career motivation. Some people are frightened by the word fifty, for it marks definite middle age. Career oriented people are not happy admitting that the rest of the world may see them as middle-aged. As a matter of fact, in some places in this country, anyone over fifty is considered a senior citizen!

At fifty, we know the company is going to begin to move us out if we work for the average corporation. This means we should make some plans—alternatives—in case the company decides to force us into early retirement. For those who are self-employed, a change of pace or a change of responsibilities is on the way. This is the time to reap recognition benefits, for most professionals are just coming into their own now. Professionals now have the experience to offer themselves as teachers for the younger people coming up. If we don't value our knowledge and experience, we may feel insecure.

This seems to be a really interesting time for women. Sheehy reports in *Pathfinders* that this is a "comeback decade" for them. The first signs of menopause can bring on feelings of insecurity. The fact that many women are just now re-entering the work world can also contribute to feelings of insecurity. However, in their late forties, women begin to assert themselves more. As Sheehy points out, women drop the "happyface masks...break the seal on repressed anger...overcome habits of trying to be perfect...and of needing to make everyone love them." What she is saying is that this is the time to develop what some people call eccentricity—or personality. Finally you can say what you want to.

So can men. Men who find they have worked for years to support the needs of the children can finally break away. This may indicate the breaking point of a marriage that lasted "for the sake of the children," as the new Jupiter return hands the responsibilities of childrearing over to the already reared child. How long must a parent be responsible for having a child? Although the child may say he's independent, that issue may not turn out to be quite true, for when the parents pull away, it may not be the parents who are uptight! These issues certainly come to light when a marriage is ended and parents go their separate ways.

For those who stay married, and who still get rid of the kids, this is a time when many suburbanites move back to the city, take a small apartment, and start living all over again. Many parents gave up the delights and enjoyments of city living in order to raise kids with a backyard. This doesn't mean that the parents *liked* living in the suburbs and commuting back and forth everyday—it may have been done as part of the parent trip. Now Mom and Dad are free to move into the city and develop anew. If the wife returns to work, her combined income may help her husband feel more comfortable about considering a change in his job. If he hasn't really liked his work for the last few years, the late forties and early fifties may mark a period of change; he can begin to develop some other work interests.

Sheehy also mentions the health and sexuality issues. These are years when the appreciation of life is reconsidered as health and well-being become important. Many people start taking better care of themselves physically. Many experience menopause—both men and women. A lot has been written in regard to female menopause, and it has been a subject of derision for years—women have sometimes been accused of being "menstrual" when they get angry (especially at men) and older women are often accused of being "menopausal." Some women do experience severe changes in physical chemistry at this time, but changes blamed on the menopause may also relate to the older woman's personality. As women get older they take less "bs" from people. It is a sign of maturity, not a sign of menopause. However, when a woman doesn't respond with a great deal of warmth or consideration for a man's feelings, it may be called menopausal in the office. Women may be subconsciously responding to the fact that as people of both sexes become older, they become more equal. Bodies become more alike. Young people don't realize this, but most men develop breast cleavage as they age. By the time they're both eighty, the male and female have both become quite rounded!

The male menopause signifies a different response. It probably is more misunderstood because it hasn't been talked about until recently in our society. Men become depressed; they are tired in the morning; they may feel aches and pains and worry about heart disease and the like. They feel a change in sex drive. The key here is that the sex drive is *changing*, not *going*. The sex drive never leaves; the only thing that stops people from enjoying sex is their own attitude about it.

Age 51-55
First Jupiter Square Jupiter (Fifth Cycle)
Jupiter Opposite Jupiter (Fifth Cycle)

This is not usually a rough time. As the fifth Jupiter cycle has already begun, we now respond to our initial relating decisions for the cycle. Most women feel quite comfortable. Those who are back in the work world really enjoy it, perhaps reaping the benefits earned from returning to school in their forties. Women who are just breaking into the work world for the first time are also happy about it. Now that the word fifty has been faced, women begin to enjoy this phase of life.

The first square will bring two months of reconsideration. Decisions made at the Jupiter conjunction need to be evaluated, and maybe one of them will be that sending the kids away wasn't so traumatic as Mom first supposed it would be. Men find that people still like them even though they are over fifty, and this period of life can be enjoyed like life has never been enjoyed before.

If you have parents that have lived to a ripe old age, this is the time when they begin to get sick and die. A change in family status is taking place, and the letting-go-of-the-kids process is making more and more sense.

Many women become grandmothers now and appreciate the prospect of seeing the family grow. For some reason, women are usually comfortable with the idea of becoming a grandmother, and enjoy helping daughters or daughters-in-law with new children. Men still involved with career may be frightened of becoming grandfathers as they don't want the stigma of age to affect work. The advent of grandchildren serves as an incentive to help the fifty-year-old realize that aging is actually a natural process. The cycle that started at age forty-eight or so has now been fulfilled. The grandparent role forces the adult into the next life stage. The youth of old age is a preparation period. For single people, the next generation doesn't serve as an instigator of future life, so they have to make this adjustment on their own. The path to aging is one we take alone, and each person will have to find it.

The Jupiter opposition lets you know how your forty-eight-year-old decision was; if you walked the right path for yourself, the last half of the cycle marks a period of growth and enjoyment. At the opposition, the person afraid of aging will buy new hair, new teeth, new eyes, maybe new ears, and new clothes, all geared to looking younger than he or she is. When you counsel someone dressed like a teenybopper, you know that age is probably a frightening prospect; unless this individual gets good counseling, the upcoming years may be uncomfortable.

Age 55-60
Last Jupiter Square Jupiter (Fifth Cycle)
Jupiter Conjunct Jupiter (Sixth Cycle)
Saturn Conjunct Saturn (Third Cycle)
Last Uranus Square Uranus (First Cycle)

You know that the pressure is on again as soon as you see Uranus looming on the scene. There are several issues needing to be handled now. First, if the grandparent phase wasn't accepted at age forty-eight, something will come along to force you to let go of your adult children. It's time to let them go—to let your kids do the cooking on Thanksgiving Day. It's okay to come to dinner and it's not necessary that "old mother" cook for everyone—let the young folks do the work. Part of letting go of the parent role is allowing your own children to become adults; if you don't let go, you may be robbing them of adulthood. A matriarch is not a cook, she is an advisor. A patriarch doesn't support his children on an allowance anymore, he is a philosopher. Your new role cannot develop if you still look back to the old days trying to recreate a family scene that no longer exists.

At the beginning of the third Saturn cycle a new birth is at hand. A new level of responsibility needs to be considered. The second Saturn cycle (age twenty-eight) brought in a period of responsibility that you never had before. It was the kind of responsibility that we were trained to look forward to by our parents. It was time to marry, raise a family, establish a home, develop a career, and support the family you created. This was an active time mainly dedicated to being part of the herd. For those who had little herd instinct, it was time to develop into being either the leader of the herd or a hunter. All our activities through our thirties, forties and early fifties relate to strengthening society or the tribe.

The third Saturn cycle brings a different kind of responsibility. In earlier generations it was significant of the rise of the statesman, the elder advisor, strong people in politics and church. Men became counselors. Well, we've been raised to become self-responsible, but few of us have been raised to become considerate of the world at large. If we have no training in this issue, we must train ourselves. The man who enters this Saturn cycle must find another place for himself, begin to think about giving up his position and become an advisor, for his knowledge in this capacity can be very useful to others.

However, it is more common to see men grasping at straws, worrying about jobs, trying to hang onto the old ways and not letting anything new into consciousness. In some cases, men are so insecure that you just can't talk to them. This may be the beginning of a very unattractive state of mind, for the man who is afraid of moving into the next cycle wants to stay in the old position. If you talk to him about change, he gets stubborn and won't listen. This stance may have sparked some companies to institute a mandatory retirement at age fifty-five or sixty, because it can be difficult to work with frightened aging people. If the company wants to add to the staff, the older men feel inadequate. It doesn't matter that the job description has changed, or that the company now handles its business by computer, or that the company has grown. Some older men need help because of changes in company business, but they feel if they ask for help they must be failures. So they work harder and longer, and still wind up behind. More insecurity is engendered because the work load isn't being alleviated. This is the sign of stagnant people, those incapable of looking beyond themselves to see where they fit in the company's scheme of things.

In other cases, men who have started the third Saturn cycle have moved to different jobs within a company, or to a related business that offers services in which our Saturnian individuals are experts. Younger men can't possibly outshine older executives who are capable of sharing experience. These men are able to offer a completely different kind of service to any company they work for. What kind? Well, the chances are they won't come in with a hangover from the party the night before. And they haven't stayed up til 3 AM with a new date. They come in fresh and ready to work. They have ideas to offer that are based on sound business practice, not impractical untested ideas. While younger men may look to balance the books or find a cheap way out, more mature executives may be interested in presenting ideas that will also be of long range benefit to the company or the company's reputation.

How do women cope with the third Saturn cycle? They may flounder for a bit, but the stress of impending old age may not be as difficult for them. At the third Saturn cycle menopause is over, the role of housewife and mother is essentially over, housekeeping takes on a completely different tone, and women can look forward to either continuing with career until retirement, or looking for a job that will offer what they look for from employment at this time in life. If these women have returned to city life at this age, they prepare to develop personal interests or partake of whatever organization or political ambitions they may have.

The important thing for all people entering this third Saturn cycle is the basis for the cycle itself. Three rounds of Saturn and most people are not on this planet anymore. Some people live till their nineties, but not many. This is a time to begin to explore the spiritual process of life—whatever that may be for you. Some become involved in whatever religious activities they wish to pursue in the community. For others, organized religion has not been a part of life up till this point, and won't be now. For those folks, I've recommended exploring Religious Science, which has a metaphysical and spiritual approach, or groups such as SFF or ARE.[15] For others, the various facets of the occult open doors to a different kind of religious/spiritual experience, and some may start by studying astrology, become drawn to the tarot, and eventually move to something more philosophical such as alchemy or qabalah. The works of Jung have been of great value to people who are looking for another path, and the works of Joseph Campbell (especially his *Hero With a Thousand Faces*) have opened new doors to consciousness for many.

If the sixth Jupiter conjunct Jupiter takes place while the Saturn cycle is also in effect, some profound changes will be made. At the beginning of this new cycle, both men and women are pushed to consider themselves in a different light. The sixth cycle concentrates on spiritual or philosophical development, and each individual will open up according to the concepts accepted during the two-month period when Jupiter is in effect. If philosophical development is avoided, this may be the start of an uncomfortable phase of life. If this cycle is explored with enthusiasm, getting older will have a great deal of meaning.

This may be a time to explore the hero's path, especially if some good reading is done beforehand. Jungian analysts are trained to work with the concept of the hero's journey, and people don't have to be considered neurotic to explore this path. Jung's own personal self-discovey was fascinating for me, and I recommend reading his

---

[15]Religious Science, or Science of Mind, has offices in most major cities. Many metaphysical bookstores carry the works of Raymond Charles Barker, Ernest Holmes, Alice Steadman, and others in the field. Most Religious Science churches also have a bookstore. If there is no organization near you, write the New York Office at 14 E. 48th St., New York, N.Y. 10017, and ask for a booklist so you can buy through the mail. You may also want to ask if there is a branch office near you.

Memories, Dreams and Reflections.[16] His perspective was wonderful as he moved through his own life, and some of his observations can be helpful at this stage of the journey.

> Our life is like the course of the sun. In the morning the sun gains continually in strength until it blazes forth in the zenith-heat of high noon; then comes the enantiodromia: its continued movement forward does not mean an increase but a decrease in strength. Thus our task in handling young people is different than that presented by people who are getting on in years.
>
> ...But it is a great error to assume that the meaning of life is exhausted in the period of sexual youth and growth; that, for example, a woman who has passed the menopause is 'finished.' The afternoon of life is just as full of meaning as the morning, only its meaning and purpose is a wholly different one. Man has two aims: the first is the aim of nature, the begetting of children and all the business of protecting the brood; to this period belongs the gaining of money and social position. When this aim is satisfied, there begins another phase, namely, that of culture.
>
> For the attainment of the former goal we have the help of nature, and moreover of education; but little or nothing helps us towards the latter goal. Indeed, often a false ambition survives, in that an old man wants to be a youth again, or at least feels he must behave like one, although within himself he can no longer make believe. It is this that makes the transition from the natural to the cultural phase terribly difficult and bitter for many people....They cling to the illusions of youth, or at least to their children, in order to preserve in this way a fragment of illusion. One sees this in mothers, who find in their children their only justification, and who imagine they have to sink away into empty nothingness when they give them up. It is no wonder, then, that many bad neuroses develop at the beginning of the afternoon of life....But the problems which appear in this age are no longer to be solved by the old rules; the hand of the clock cannot be turned back; what youth found and must find outside, the man of middle life must find within himself.[17]

The Saturn cycle at this stage is representative of the fourth cycle in the Hindu life system. Not that the Hindus do it anymore. But for the sake of perspective, let's discuss this ancient system for a moment. The first cycle is that of being a child, the second indicates student years, the third is the householder (keeping a home, raising a family, and taking care of parents), and the fourth is devoted to spiritual development. At the fourth cycle, no older person is

[16]See *Memories, Dreams and Reflections*, C. J. Jung, recorded and edited by Aniela Jaffe, translated from the German by R. and C. Winston, Pantheon Books, New York, 1961. The book is also available in paper.

[17]See *Two Essays on Analytical Psychology*, C. G. Jung, translated by H. G. and C. F. Baynes, Dodd, Mead & Co., New York, 1928, pp. 77, 78. Used by permission.

required to do anything for anyone else. Possessions were given away, family was left behind, and the aging person went off into the hills to find illumination. Whether Hindu or Buddhist, the Oriental personality is receptive to the idea of reincarnation. It must be prepared for or you won't be ready when you die. This sounds like a really good idea, for the concept is supportive of the older person and the needs of the entire life span. We can do it in this culture too. We don't have to go off into the woods or use a begging bowl, but we can leave ourselves open to the experience of a spiritual opening in later life. We can consider growing old a privilege and an honor.

The oriental way has a built in system for respecting the elderly, according to Erwin Rousselle. He says that in order to explore the tradition of contemporary Taoism, one must reach a certain age. The Chinese have a

> ...strong feeling for the stages of inner growth of man. It is reflected in their customs. The man of forty, usually already a grandfather, is entitled to grow a mustache; the man of sixty, who is often a great-grandfather, is permitted a full beard. The spiritual clarity of complete detachment is similarly associated with age. A man must be close to forty before he is instructed in the meditation of the backward-flowing movement; only at the approach of sixty does a man dedicate himself entirely to the "tao of heaven" (t'ien tao).[18]

The Uranus square is working at this time as well. The planet is significant in symbolizing the individuation process. At the first square, we were pushed out of our childhood home to join the adult community. At the opposition we wanted to turn life upside down and start all over. Now we need another push to start looking at the next phase of life and how we will live it. We walked into young adulthood with very little knowledge and experience. We can walk into old age in the same ignorant fashion, or we can try to prepare ourselves for what is ahead.

Exploring the concept of death is one that may help people live, for if we look at it and prepare for it, we don't have to do it. Life can be enjoyable for no shadow is lurking behind us, waiting to take us unaware. Elisabeth Kübler-Ross[19] has written a lot about the death

---

[18]See *Spiritual Disciplines, Papers from the Eranos Yearbooks*, 4, edited by Joseph Campbell, Bollingen Series XXX, Pantheon Books, New York, 1960. Erwin Rousselle contributed a paper called "Spiritual Guidance in Contemporary Taoism" (1933), p. 95.

[19]See *Questions and Answers on Death and Dying*, Elisabeth Kübler-Ross, MacMillan Publishing Co., New York, 1974; and *Death: The Final Stage of Growth*, Prentice Hall, A Spectrum Book, Englewood Cliffs, N.J., 1974.

experience and how it relates to the nursing and caring professions. She has also discussed the reactions that take place within the individual who is approaching death. The other concept worth exploring is how you intend to leave this world. A very loving and spiritually aware book for people who are curious about their last moments is Debbie Duda's *Guide to Dying at Home*.[20] When I was reading this book and recommending it to people in the helping professions, I was asked if I was planning on dying! My response to that fear was "It's okay to read books about natural childbirth, but it's not *natural* to read books about the process of death?" We live an entire lifetime knowing that we are going to die someday, but no one wants to look at the prospect. The more we run from it, the bigger the shadow of death becomes in our psyches.

The Uranus square also brings with it the development of eccentricity. Older people are free to say more, do more, and take less. Insights and comments made by older folks are refreshing. Or stodgy and bitter. The choice is yours. As one author put it, "If you want to stay young, the first thing you do is throw away all the baby pictures of your grandchildren."[21] He said that showing baby pictures, doting on grandchildren, and being adoring grandparents was one of the most boring things that anyone could do if you are interested in staying open and alive mentally. No one cares what your grandchildren look like; people care about what you look like, what you are doing, and how you are spending your time.

Age 61-64
First Jupiter Square Jupiter (Sixth Cycle)
Jupiter Opposite Jupiter (Sixth Cycle)
Maybe Uranus Square Uranus (First Cycle)

During this period, the primary urges of development will revolve around Jupiter, and these are short-term cycles that only last for a couple of months. The changes that will become apparent are

---

[20]See *Guide to Dying at Home*, Debbie Duda, John Muir Publications, Santa Fe, N.M. 87501, to be reissued in 1984 under the new title, *Coming Home: A Guide to Home Care for the Terminally Ill.*

[21]I have absolutely no idea who wrote that. I think it was the first line in a book about how to stay young. That may even be the title. The line stuck in my head and I couldn't resist using it here, but it isn't my idea. What do you say about a baby picture except, "That's nice! What a lovely baby!" And you have to say it, even if the kid is ugly, which some of them are.

related to how you started the sixth Jupiter cycle. It's the letting go stage. If you haven't begun to let go, circumstances will arise that will push you to let go, or you'll begin to feel more and more uncomfortable. At the Jupiter opposition, you'll know how this is working, for you will either have difficulties at that time (meaning you didn't let go) or you will be rewarded, and will find that the decisions you are making are enhancing your inner feeling of self-worth.

This is the retirement age for sure. Many people are in the midst of a whole new lifestyle because of retirement. They move from one place to another. Others are forced to make new relating changes as they move from a daily work load to a retirement program. It's important to have a program, for if retirement signals boredom and no outside interests, it may not be long before death is a constant companion.

If the Jupiter square and opposition don't push the change in awareness, maybe the Uranus square will. People need counseling now, for to miss out on the development phase of this third Saturn cycle will cause a lot of unnecessary fear and anguish. According to M. Esther Harding, we have to make the step for awareness and old age for ourselves:

> Most people, if they allow themselves to think about the subject at all, look forward to this period with fear and apprehension....No wonder that the majority of people put all their effort into warding off old age as long as possible. By "keeping young," and binding themselves to their children and to their work activities, they hope to hold on to life as they have known it during the years of their strength....But in trying to keep up with the times and the younger generation, they really lag behind their own generation, they fail to keep up with their own time....Up to the beginning of the twentieth century, old people had a recognized place in the family circle. Today this is no longer so. Each individual man and woman must now face old age, with its difficulties and necessary adjustments, for himself.

> In the Gothic period later life was reserved for religious developments; after the heat and struggle of the day was over, men and women turned their attention to making their peace with God through prayer and meditation. Culture of the inner life was recognized as the specific task of the old, more especially if their active years had been passed in entirely secular occupations.

> Old age can no longer be considered a tribal problem, no longer a family problem, no longer a religious problem taken into account by society at large through the maintenance of retreats and monasteries. The problem of old age is today principally a personal one which each

individual must solve for himself, and its solution is hardly to be hoped
for if preparation is delayed too long.[22]

Essentially she is saying that we must become responsible for the last
years of our life, as the social structure doesn't provide for us. In this
new age of consciousness, the barriers are removed from the caste (or
social) system, but instead of being taken care of, as we were in a
tightly knit caste society, we are now free to make our own
decisions—and that freedom brings with it the responsibility of
having to think for ourselves.

Age 65-70
Last Jupiter Square Jupiter (Sixth Cycle)
Jupiter Conjunct Jupiter (Seventh Cycle)
First Saturn Square Saturn (Third Cycle)

Pulling away is really the issue now. The seventh Jupiter cycle
indicates the start of a twelve-year period of intense spiritual
development, or at least the potential for it. Many of the concepts
understood now can be shared with others and the insights gained
can be valuable in an advisory sense. Learning about this spiritual
stage of life can be shared by many people if you join groups that give
you support and feedback.[23]

Saturn squaring itself may give Jupiter a push here, for the two
energies have to balance out. The change in lifestyle doesn't mean
you should cut yourself off from everyone, but it does indicate a need
to establish yourself in a different perspective. This perspective is
one that has to come from inside yourself. Retirement may still be an
issue, for many people retire at the age of sixty-five. Some are already
coping with the process for many leave the business world at sixty
and sixty-two. This may be the year to go back to work if retirement
was started early. This may be a year of stress if retirement was forced
on you by your company and you didn't make any plans. Although

---

[22]*The Way of All Women*, M. Esther Harding, Harper Colophon Books, New York,
1970, pp. 243-246. Quoted from paper edition and used by permission: in the U.S.A.,
courtesy of the C. G. Jung Foundation for Analytical Psychology, Inc., New York; in
the U.K., courtesy of the Hutchinson Publishing Co. (Rider Pocket Edition),
London.

[23]Any group in your area that sponsors spiritual retreats would be helpful. If you
don't have a local group, you can contact SFF (Spiritual Frontiers Fellowship) at
10819 Winner Rd., Independence, MO 64054, or ARE (The Association for Research
and Enlightenment), Box 595, Virginia Beach, VA 23451. Both groups have local
chapters; by joining either group you'll get notification about upcoming conferences,
seminars, and special retreats (some may be held in your neighborhood).

the third Saturn cycle recommends a change, that change doesn't mean giving up. We need our elder statesmen and stateswomen.

For those who are confused about what to do with themselves, some light reading may be available to help you open up to aging. One enjoyable book about the aging process and what we are worth as older people is *It Takes a Long Time to Become Young.*[24]

Age 70-80

Jupiter Conjunct Jupiter (Seventh Cycle)
First Jupiter Square Jupiter (Seventh Cycle)
Jupiter Opposite Jupiter (Seventh Cycle)
Saturn Opposite Saturn (Third Cycle)
Last Saturn Square Saturn (Third Cycle)
Neptune Opposite Neptune (First Cycle)
Maybe Pluto Opposite Pluto (First Cycle)

As you will notice, I'm now moving to ten-year increments because it's impossible to take these years individually. I don't know enough about how the energy will work because very little has been written about how people respond to energy during this period of life, and I haven't experienced it myself.

Observation has shown, however, that the person who remains in relatively good health, and who maintains an active interest in life and life projects, remains vital during these years. People who have neglected the spiritual development necessary to clarify their vision are immersed in thinking about visits from children and grandchildren, and are often lonely and depressed. Here Jung's insight is helpful, for he sums up what has to be said at this phase:

> If he is to live, he must fight and sacrifice his longing for the past in order to rise to his own heights. After having reached the noonday heights, he must sacrifice his love for his own achievement, for he may not loiter. The sun, too, sacrifices its greatest strength in order to hasten on to the fruits of autumn, which are the seeds of rebirth.... we soon discover that this praiseworthy and apparently unavoidable battle with the years leads to stagnation and dessication of soul. Our convictions become platitudes ground out on a barrel-organ, our ideals become starchy habits, enthusiasm stiffens into automatic gestures. The source of the water of life seeps away. We ourselves may not notice it, but everybody else does, and that is even more painful. If we should risk a little introspection, coupled perhaps with an energetic attempt to be honest for once with ourselves, we may get a dim idea of all the wants,

---

[24]See *It Takes a Long Time to Become Young*, Garson Kanin, Berkeley Books, New York, 1979, paperback.

longings, and fears that have accumulated down there—a repulsive and
sinister sight. The mind shies away, but life wants to flow down into
the depths....Everything young grows old, all beauty fades, all heat
cools, all brightness dims, and every truth becomes stale and trite. For
all these things have taken on shape, and all shapes are worn thin by the
working of time; they age, sicken, crumble to dust—unless they change.
But change they can, for the invisible spark that generated them is
potent enough for infinite generation.[25]

If nothing was done about the third Saturn cycle in the late fifties,
then the Saturn opposition will take its toll in the seventies. When
Jung talks of changing with the times, he is also talking of
regression. He says, "For life goes on despite loss of youth; indeed it
can be lived at the greatest intensity if looking back at what is
already moribund does not hamper your step."[26] He says that people
tend to go back into childhood memories, to regress into memories
of the past. Because of what he says, I wonder if early senility, or
senility in general, has some relationship with the psychological
regression of which Jung speaks, namely a fear of going forward.
Jung said that childhood memories are also mixed with magical
images that are intuitively gained from the collective unconscious.
And to lose oneself in these images is to totally withdraw from the
world. If the libido is locked in, and not given a chance to become
mature or conscious at this stage of life, it must go somewhere, and
it pulls the individual into the labyrinth of unconscious *prima
materia*. And of course, the pull is in the wrong direction because
the aging consciousness is lost.

Another confrontation that could be symbolized by the Saturn
opposition was shown in the film *On Golden Pond*. We rarely have
an opportunity to experience such an intimate closeness with two
older people. We certainly don't get to experience this with our
parents, and most older people don't get a chance to discuss it with
each other. To watch the wife celebrate spring in her ritual dance,
and to watch her husband withdraw into his fascination about death
was a privilege. At one point Katherine Hepburn asks, "Why are you
thinking about dying all the time?" and Henry Fonda replies, "It's

[25]See *The Collected Works of C. G. Jung*, trans. R.F.C. Hull, Bollingen Series 20,
Vol. 5: *Symbols of Transformation*. Copyright © 1956 by Princeton University Press.
Excerpt, pp. 356-7. Used by permission of Princeton University Press, U.S.A., and
Routledge Kegan Paul, U.K.

[26]See *The Collected Works of C.G. Jung*, Trans. R.F.C. Hull, Bollingen Series 20,
Vol. 5: *Symbols of Transformation*, Princeton University Press, 1956, p. 408.

the most interesting thing I can think about." Once he experienced his brush with death, a certain kind of energy was released and you know at the end of the movie that it doesn't matter when he dies, for he will now live until he does.

Age 80-90
Jupiter Conjunct Jupiter (Eighth Cycle)
Saturn Conjunct Saturn (Fourth Cycle)
Uranus Conjunct Uranus (Second Cycle)
Neptune Opposite Neptune (First Cycle)
Pluto Opposite Pluto (First Cycle)

This was considered the end of life. The cycles will all vary based on your year of birth, and the combination of cycles will mark the end of life or a new beginning of experience. It might be appropriate to tie the end of life into the Cabalistic Tree of Life. As Halevi says, this tree has been with us for two thousand years and every age sees it through their eyes. He discusses the tree in all its symbolic phases, and says of the aging process:

> Binah [Mother] is old age. Contrary to the usual belief that this period is a terminal one of running down, it is a preparation for the dynamic of the birth of death. Certainly the body is decaying and all the vital processes are sluggish, but the invisible part of man that inhabits this physical shell is, or should be, full of a lifetime's experience. While the body can no longer run a mile, usually an unnecessary accomplishment in old age, the soul can ponder on the material collected over the years. Silence and stillness are all that are needed. A good head and heart, backed up by a slowly clearing memory of earlier times so characteristic of old age, can review life, and come to an understanding not possible in a busy outward existence. Time is the quality of Binah, whose traditional planet is Saturn.[27]

And with this I end this section. If the material on aging is helpful to anyone who reads this, I would like to hear about it. The opportunity and the glory of the aging process is just beginning to be written about in this age. We have a fantastic future to look forward to as we begin to work with the concept of consciousness and aging, knowing that in years to come our aging can bring on a personal consciousness and awareness that was once reserved only for holy men.

---

[27]See *An Introduction to the Cabala*, Z'ev ben Shimon Halevi, Samuel Weiser, Inc., York Beach, ME 03910, 1972, p. 159.

Since ev'ry man who lives is born to die,
And none can boast sincere felicity
With equal mind, what happens, let us bear,
Nor joy nor grieve too much for things beyond our care.
Like pilgrims to th' appointed place we tend;
The world's an inn, and death the journey's end.

John Dryden
Palamon and Arcite, Book 3

PART 3

COUNSELING A CRISIS

Two roads diverged in a wood, and I—
I took the one less traveled by,
And that has made all the difference.
Robert Frost
The Road Not Taken

Every session with a client will be different. The astrologer may understand full well how to interpret the cycles of life and the transits (or progressions) that activate the natal chart, but no astrologer can know ahead of time exactly what a meeting with a client will bring about. Each person's chart is a blueprint of possible life experience. How any individual has responded to previous cycles and transits cannot be known, and the session you have today will be founded on decisions the client made years ago.

The sample reading that follows illustrates how cycles can be integrated with the reading of the natal chart and what the astrologer needs to think about in the process of synthesizing the information available about the client. This section is included because many students have expressed concern about doing readings. After learning basic interpretation and all the formulas for working with progressions or transits, the big problem remaining is, how to approach a real live person? How much information do you discuss? Who runs the session? What if you get into a session that's over your head? Usually, adequate preparation and an understanding of when to shut up will help you avoid unpleasant situations.

I'm not going to define a lot of terms in this section because it would be repetitive. My basic outlook about the natal chart is discussed in my first book, *Astrological Insights into Personality*, and my views on transits and how I use them are presented in *Transits: The Time of Your Life*. There are many other books on the market that can aid you in learning the basics of interpretation, and you probably already have formulated your own ideas.

When preparing for a session, I do the natal chart and then the transits and cycles. Before the client arrives, I've looked at the natal chart to determine what might be going on with this person. In order to prepare myself adequately, I have to run a lot of possibilities through my head, so that I'm ready to discuss any potential issues that may arise. By considering a wide range of possibilities relating to behavior symbolized by natal aspects, I can be better prepared to ask the right questions; sometimes the astrologer can pick up on an issue that needs to be discussed, especially when the client isn't clear about verbalizing it.

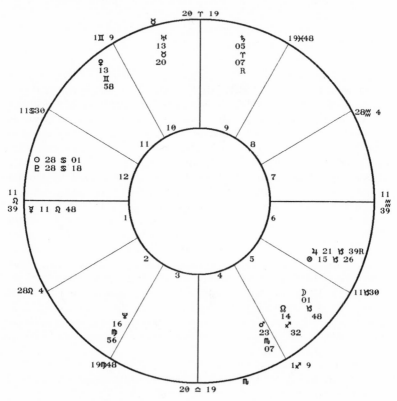

Jane's natal chart. Jane was born July 21, 1937, in England. The chart has been calculated by Astro-Computing Services in San Diego, CA, using the Placidus house system. The birth data was rectified by an American astrologer and later verified by a baby book. The details of the birth data have been withheld to protect the identity of the client. Chart used with permission.

We start by looking at the natal chart. This chart belongs to a client who has given me permission to use it. Her name has been changed to protect her identity; the information presented here is true. Following the natal chart, a section has been included to provide the client's actual background, so that you can see the difference between looking at the chart of an unknown personality and how that energy actually manifests in a real person. Then we discuss her transits and cycles, and conclude the section with a report on what was an issue during the first session with this client.

THE NATAL CHART

Jane's natal chart appears on page 140. A complete delineation of her chart is not within the scope of this book; however, we will take a brief look at how the planets and aspects might be working so you can understand what the transits (or progressions) will activate in her personality structure. Please keep in mind that every astrologer interprets a chart differently, and you may see things in this chart that I haven't mentioned. (What you see may well be something that is an important issue to the client, so don't ignore your own impressions.) Also bear in mind that it is utterly impossible to completely "read" anyone's chart in one session; the symbolism contained in a natal chart can be discussed for weeks on end, and the client can't handle that much information in one session.

I look at *where* the Sun is placed before I do anything else. Jane's Sun is in the 12th house, indicating a personality that is not completely visible to an observer. The 12th house placement tells me that she probably gets involved with other people's burdens and needs, and she may not adequately take care of her own needs. She may also have a private life, be a very secluded type, or may not share important thoughts easily with others, and we might try to explore these issues during the session.

It's important to notice how many planets are above and below the horizon. In my experience, I've found that I must be more careful with the words I choose and about how much information I present when most of the planets are above the horizon. So before I talk, I want to see what I need to do with this client. The balance of energy in Jane's chart is equally divided: she has five planets above and five below the horizon. This indicates a certain amount of stability and receptivity, and that I won't have to watch my words quite as carefully as if she had, for instance, eight planets above the horizon.

I want to stress the fact that *words* are terribly important when an astrologer tries to communicate with another human being. We have no way of knowing how our choice of words will affect a client, or what "buttons" our words will activate. We have our own set of key words that can convey a complicated image to us. Mention Saturn conjunct the Moon to an astrologer and you eliminate the need to discuss the whole image. But these symbolic images are not a part of the client's experience, and we may need to explain something in a very different way to communicate with a client. I have found myself exhausted after a session, not because astrology is difficult, but because the right choice of words was so important. And frankly, I haven't always done as well as I could have.

The next thing we want to look at is the balance of planets on the east and west side of the chart so that we can see the kind of energy Jane has at her disposal and determine to some degree whether she is a "go-getter" or "receiver" of experience. Other factors will influence this decision, but here we will consider how many planets appear in houses 10 through 3 (going counter-clockwise) versus how many appear in houses 4 through 9 inclusive. It seems to me that when most of the planets are in houses 10 through 3, the individual takes charge of her life, and if you crack the door open for her, she will be able to make the necessary changes, as soon as she discovers they can be done. When most of the planets are in houses 4 through 9, the individual is more of a team player, one who may need to work within the framework of a group. Jane has six planets in houses 10 through 3, which indicates that she is able to change and can initiate changes on her own.

The triplicities and quadruplicities will indicate more about her interests,[1] and will help me discover what she will respond to when I talk with her. Jane's quadruplicities work out as follows:

Cardinal 5
Fixed 3
Mutable 2

Cardinal signs symbolize action, so with five planets in cardinal signs, she will solve her problems by taking action, and she has a lot of energy to do it. If something stops her from taking action on an outer level, you will see quite an intense person. She may not take action the way others would take action since her action planet

---

[1]For an interesting discussion of triplicities and quadruplicities, see *The Neptune Effect*, Patricia Morimando. Samuel Weiser, Inc., York Beach, ME, 1979.

(Mars) is in a water sign, plus she's a Cancer Sun sign. She will take her own kind of action, and it might look as though she's moving sideways. She may also take action before thinking through its consequences (because of natal aspects we'll discuss later), so I would be looking to see manifestations of this when we talk.

The three planets in fixed signs indicate a certain amount of stability, and she is "fixed" enough to be able to carry through on projects if she wants to. She has only two mutable planets, so she may not be too open to the idea of change. Mutables indicate our ability to change, whether we can be open to new ideas, whether or not we can be responsive to ideas suggested by others—and this is her weakest area. We need to look at the quadruplicities to see which ones are over- and under-represented, as this gives us a clue to where the balance is out of kilter. The issue in this chart is between cardinal and mutable concepts: her cardinal count takes action too quickly, while mutable is a little under-represented and so she may not listen as much as she could.

The triplicities are the next issue, and their balance needs to be considered in relation to her personal planets to see how she responds to herself as well as to others. Usually we become self-conscious of what we have too much of, and we are hungry to increase our level of whatever it is we lack. Knowing this can help us understand what Jane seeks and values, as well as where she will try to develop herself.

Fire 2	Air 1
Earth 4	Water 3

Jane has two fire planets, and a lack of fire tends to need an awful lot of attention from others. A zero fire person can be quite demanding, while someone with two fire needs some attention but it isn't an overwhelming need. She is a Cancer person though and needs loving attention, but she isn't maniacal about it. She has four earth planets, so she feels quite stable inside. It's important to note that she won't be impressed by money, clothing, or material acquisitions, although she is capable of enjoying such things. People who have a lot of earth can enjoy life but won't sell their souls for it, as might someone with no earth. The balance of earth may be something to discuss because she may have been accused of not appreciating gifts; and if she has marital or relationship problems, other people may be trying to show their love by buying her things when in fact she doesn't want them.

The one air planet indicates that she doesn't think she has enough intellect. This setup often manifests in a quite capable mind, for when we seek to develop what we think we lack, we make it stronger. People with few air planets are usually more intellectual and more curious about learning new things than are people with a great deal of air. The other issue here is that she may not trust her intellect, and she may think she's dumb or too emotional, or whatever.

The three water planets indicate a fairly normal balance. She's quite sensitive to her own feelings as well as the feelings of others. She may be a bit nervous about expressing her emotions because of a fear of being hurt. Notice that the water planets are Sun, Mars, and Pluto, and because Pluto is conjunct her Sun (this will be discussed later) she may need to talk about a fear of expressing herself emotionally.

The next thing I want to think about before looking at her aspects is the trinity of personality: Sun, Moon, and ascendant. How these configurations relate to each other by sign and quality will give additional color to the personality we are about to study. The Sun is in a water sign in the 12th house. The Sun represents the "I am" factor of the personality, and she will manifest some version of the traits commonly assigned to Cancer. For example, Cancerians are sometimes known as homebodies, and Cancer women are often considered good cooks. I don't agree with this kind of diagnosis at all, because these are Cancerian *issues*, not *facts*. Some Cancerians build a nest and never leave it; others create a comfortable home and are never there; others don't want a home. Some Cancerian women like to cook and are good at it; others can't cook or hate it. The issue in common for Cancers involves a response to food and housing, which goes beyond normal interest in the subject. Cancerians are also concerned with issues about parenting; some like being parents and some hate it; some are good parents and others are not. So my conclusion would be that she has a strong Cancerian background and I don't know how she's using this energy.

We add to the Sun symbolism by noting how her feeling nature will express itself. The Moon is in the sign of Capricorn, a sign known for its traditional values. Capricorn is associated with management, control, and organization. It is also an earth sign, and as such, the Moon will have an "earthy" quality to it. The Moon indicates "I feel" and we compare it to the "I am" of the Sun; the two facets of personality have to express together in one person. Although there is no opposition (by aspect) between the Sun and the

Moon, the Cancer-Capricorn components will be an issue in her personality. How do you "manage" your feelings? How can you be an emotionally oriented Cancer type when your Moon says that isn't such a good idea?

Sun is in water, Moon is in earth. Earth and water are mutually beneficial qualities, for earth needs water in order to be fertile. Rain can do wonders for the earth on one hand, but it can also erode the soil and wash it away. The Sun is in a water sign, and the Sun represents the ideological framework of the personality. The Moon in an earth sign symbolizes the physical body as well as the way Jane responds to life. In her case, the water of the Sun is lapping at the shores of the Moon. She may be afraid that her Sun self is able to erode her feeling responses. If the Moon is afraid of the Sun (earth afraid of water), she may be apprehensive about dealing with personal feelings or responses. The emotional nature of the Cancer Sun may cause her Capricorn Moon a great deal of pain and vice versa.

The Sun and Moon are both covered up by the Leo ascendant. The ascendant represents the persona, or the "face" that we show the world. Jane's trinity of personality is water and earth, with a fire sign representing her in public. The Cancer emotionality and sensitivity will be represented up front by idealistic Leo, a sign that needs to be properly respected, a sign that is proud and sensitive to any kind of criticism. Leo is involved with a lot of "shoulds" and "shouldn'ts," and these qualities will work more easily with those of the Moon, indicating that the 12th house Sun may have to be quite mature (in age) before being able to express itself and its needs.

Before meeting her, I would wonder if Jane is a woman who is in an unfulfilling marriage or job, based on the probability that she was in her late twenties before beginning to express her Sun nature. Family responsibilities or commitments might also inhibit her development by keeping her from learning to express herself. I would also wonder what she did with herself when the Cancer traits overrode the ascendant traits. Would she embarrass herself? And if so, how would she do it, and what effect would her behavior ultimately have on her lifestyle? Or would the Cancer traits be submerged by the combination of Leo and Capricorn energy? Would there be a "small unloved child" inside her that would really need encouragement to develop? Before meeting and talking with her, I wouldn't know. I would be readying myself to notice anything that would give me a lead as to how she is responding to her potential.

Now let's look more closely at her Sun. It's in Cancer and this indicates a whole set of personality traits.[2] She may be a person who was strongly influenced by her mother when she was little, and she may have a strong investment in being maternal (or not), or in being superfeminine (or not).[3] She may protect herself by playing several roles, including that of "big momma" or "little girl," and the chances are she is quite powerful. Her power may not be visible because her Sun is in the 12th house, and water power from a Cancerian type is sometimes hard for others to see.

There are aspects to the Sun, and now we need to see what's going on there. The biggest natal aspect to the Sun is its conjunction to Pluto. This conjunction indicates a number of possible manifestations of personality. She may not know why she is motivated to do what she does or why she is the person she is. She may also be a very controlled (or controlling) person, which means (in plain English) that she may be a highly manipulative type. She may also be inordinately talented, for Pluto symbolizes a natural tie to the collective unconscious of humanity, and she may be able to manifest this energy in a constructive and creative manner. If she is able to funnel the energy through to consciousness, we don't know what kind of person she may be. If she hasn't manifested the energy, it may be using her by blocking her growth and perceptions, so that she is merely trying to hang on to whatever it is she values. She may be involved in the process of what Jung called individuation,

---

[2]For a complete discussion on Sun types, see my book *Astrological Insights into Personality*. Astro-Computing Services, San Diego, CA, 1980. Or use your own interpretation of the Cancer type here.

[3]Feminine in the Cancerian sense is very hard for me to put into words, so I beg my reader's indulgence while I try to communicate a feeling response. Superfeminine is a word I use to describe a woman who needs to project sexuality in order to confirm the fact that she is a woman—someone who is *always* dressed to the hilt, *always* wearing make-up, *always* well-groomed, *always* aware of the feminine presentation. (It's not unusual for a woman to care about her appearance—I'm talking about the woman who obviously overdoes this.) It can indicate a woman who never lets you forget that she has breasts, or hips, or legs, and her body will be as much a part of her conversation as her voice, whether she talks with men or women. It can also signify a woman who is so self-conscious of her feminine self that she buries it under layers of fat in order to keep the rest of the world from seeing her. And added to this concept is an energy that is sometimes related to the Earth Mother type, the woman who becomes overwhelming in her anxiousness to take care of your needs. This woman may try to solve all your problems, feed you more food than you want, and overpower any budding ideas that you have so you don't allow yourself to develop any feelings of self-confidence. Excessive mothering can be related to a strong Pluto aspect, or it can be significant when Cancer or Scorpio planets play a prominent role in the chart.

finding out who she is and how she can best develop. We don't know
how any of this energy will be operating until we see her.

There is also an opposition between the Sun and Jupiter. This
is not a less important aspect than the Pluto-Sun conjunction, but
Pluto is an overwhelming influence, and Jupiter can be handled
more easily on a conscious level, especially when the aspect is
understood. The aspect reinforces the possibility that Jane doesn't
know who she is. Jupiter, to me, indicates how we reach out to
express ourselves; essentially Jupiter shows how we relate to the
universe around us, how we open up to new people, new ideas, new
concepts of self. Jupiter indicates how we relate to others, but more
importantly, how we relate to the various facets of our own
personalities. Jupiter in Capricorn indicates that she relates as a
Capricorn would, or in a pretty traditional manner. This means she
may not be expressing the needs of her Cancer Sun, or if she does,
she may feel guilty about it.

Jupiter is in Capricorn and so is the Moon, while the Sun
conjuncts Pluto in the 12th house. This is a big complex to work
with. Jane has had this chart all her life, so the complex is familiar
to her. Astrology students should keep in mind that this is the kind
of complex therapists would spend time on, for it indicates a great
deal of stress. A therapist would have to wait until the client reveals
some of the complex, while astrologers can look at the natal chart
and see the potential for it. The configuration seems quite simple,
but it could be discussed over several sessions since a discussion of it
will take some time: the client will need time to digest the material
being discussed.

The complex indicated by this Cancer-Capricorn configuration
may mean that sacrifices are being made in terms of expressing the
"I am" part of the self. Cancerian ideology may be held within the
personality, while the outer manifestation of personality is being
represented by Capricorn traits. All the hard aspects to the Sun
indicate something energizing itself while blocking the basic person
inside the chart. Jane may not know who she is or she may not give
herself a chance to be herself for some reason. Her reasons for not
expressing herself will come out when we talk, but the chart tells me
she should be talking about some difficulty in this area. If she
doesn't want to discuss this in the session, or if she thinks this isn't
an important issue, I would keep in mind that she may be
completely out of touch with herself (actually her inner conflicts). A
person who doesn't know how to express the self is in need of
counseling, but if the lack of ability to express is seen as a

frustration, you are dealing with a reasonably healthy individual—someone who can eventually take charge of the problem if given some understanding of it. If no difficulty is seen by the client, you may be dealing with an extremely repressed personality, someone who is so repressed that he or she doesn't even know something is wrong. These two aspects (Pluto conjunct the Sun and Jupiter opposing it) are strong enough that a woman of forty should recognize some of the manifestations. (If you find that she doesn't, you may want to recommend a more traditional therapy to the client, for repression is hard to counsel if you are not trained to do it.)

The Sun trines Saturn, which is both good and bad. All astrologers like trines, but trines may indicate tendencies to flow with the status quo of the personality, which isn't necessarily good in this case. The trine gives Jane the ability to work with authority figures, with men in general, with managerial types of situations. This signifies that she could be quite a career person if she develops in that direction. However, there are other issues to consider: if Saturn symbolizes the psychological influence of the father (during formative years), then she got along well with her father. However, I would wonder if they were the two "losers" who ganged up on Mom because Mom was the power figure at home. This concept relates to the development of Cancer traits in general, and I would wonder if she could cope with authority if it came from a woman. Would she be involved in using her "femininity" to play big momma or little girl roles, and is the Saturn trine helping her do it because she gets along so well with men? Is this trine helping her maintain the immature stuff that relates to the Cancer sign type? Or is the Saturn influence affected by the Jupiter opposition to the Sun, or is the Pluto conjunction to the Sun overwhelming the Sun-Saturn trine? If so, the trine may be an energy source that needs to be consciously developed.

Jane's Moon is in the sign of Capricorn, squaring natal Saturn. Moon in Capricorn indicates that she is an earthy type emotionally, with a healthy emotional nature, and probably earthy sexual responses. Her reaction to life, her feeling nature, and other facets of personality that are attributed to the Moon are expressed by Capricorn means. This indicates a person who responds to life in a strongly traditional way, probably trying to manage feeling responses so that they are socially acceptable. Already we are building an interesting Sun-Moon combination when we look at this chart, for the Cancer type is heavily emotional compared to other types, and the Capricorn Moon isn't going to want to express this emotion freely.

Note that the Moon squares Saturn, which indicates that Jane will be quite protective of her feelings. Another personality struggle is becoming apparent, for while the Sun trines Saturn, the Moon squares it. The Sun can work well with management, while the Moon may feel unqualified to do it. The Sun works well with people in positions of authority, while the Moon may feel apprehensive and sell itself short.

If natal Saturn signified the psychological influence of the father during the child's formative years, a duality is beginning to show itself, for her "I am" nature gets along well with her father, but he doesn't do anything to help the development of her feeling nature because Saturn squares the Moon. The Moon represents, among other things, the physical mother of the child, and the square indicates that Jane's Mom and Dad weren't the greatest couple to use as role models for achieving a fulfilling relationship. This aspect usually indicates that the father did not fill the mother's emotional needs, and the child will see this, usually absorbing the information on an unconscious level. When this takes place, a young girl will grow up to be a woman who expects very little from a relationship with a man because she believes all men are like her father, and men don't fulfill the needs of women. This can indicate a woman who tends to marry beneath herself socially, who takes more yuck stuff in a relationship than a woman who doesn't have the aspect would, and who is not comfortable taking care of her own emotional needs when these needs are not met by her partner. This is usually an unconscious behavior pattern, because the energy was absorbed by osmosis during early childhood years. The pattern can be changed with counseling, but it needs counseling. We won't know if she has handled this until we see her.

If a large orb is used when looking at this natal chart, Jane also has a Moon-Uranus trine (Moon at 1° Capricorn, Uranus at 13° Taurus).[4] If this aspect works in her chart, it indicates that she is more energetic than other Capricorn Moon types. Uranus gives her a

---

[4]Many readers know that I use a large orb when reading charts. This has been discussed previously in Part 1. Briefly, I use a ten-degree orb for hard aspects when the Sun and Moon are involved, and I will even consider using fifteen degrees. The Church of Light in California uses twelve degrees for the luminaries (Sun and Moon) when they make major aspects to other planets, and this Moon-Uranus trine is a 12° orb. Keep in mind that if the large orb is used, midpoint structures and really small aspects can't be used because the symbolism of the chart will become very confused.

creative spark that will liven up the earthy Moon, even though Uranus, too, is in an earth sign. She may have a strong creative response to life, and may intuitively come up with interesting concepts or ideas. These concepts may make her more interesting socially, as her response to life may be quick and witty, or it may be expressed in a career situation where she intuitively discovers answers to problems that need solving on the job.

We already discussed the fact that Jane has Leo rising; we now need to take into account that she has Mercury in Leo conjunct the ascendant. This aspect can indicate that she will talk about what she's doing, that she can be quite verbal. Although the Sun is in the 12th house and signifies that she can be quite secretive about certain facets of her life and personality, Mercury on the ascendant indicates that she'll talk about whatever it is she doesn't mind talking about. She may want to discuss issues about which she is conscious, for she has already solved the problem she is revealing. It may be a tricky session if you listen to her, for it may seem that she has it all together. It will be important to note if she wants to talk about the problems she hasn't solved. The 12th house planets are hard to bring to consciousness, and when you can't "name" your problem you can't solve it. So I will be listening to hear whether or not she is avoiding something.

We need to keep in mind that Jane has Mercury at 11° Leo and Uranus at 13° Taurus. Under certain conditions, she can become a blabbermouth—talking too much, and essentially betraying her own need to be respected (Leo). Why a blabbermouth? On the one hand, Uranus quickens the mind and the communication faculties, and on the other (especially with hard aspects) it causes one to talk when discretion would be better. I don't know why this happens, but Mercury-Uranus ties tend to cause the native to become an honorary Sagittarian at times, inserting a foot in the mouth by saying too much at the wrong time. I've also noticed that this "foot-in-mouth" disease is hard to cure, for as the individual tries to bail herself out of the mess she's made, she digs herself in deeper. (Gerald Ford has the opposition.)

Leo rising may cause Jane to appear rather fiery. I would also keep in mind that Leo is a sign that symbolizes quite a "proper" group of people, as does her Capricorn Moon. She may, therefore, be more involved with tradition and "proper behavior" than with the more outgoing traits attributed to Leo. Underneath her persona (the facade she offers to the general public) may exist a person who really wants to be respected more than anything else. In some cases when

Leo planets are afflicted, the individual believes so strongly that no respect is forthcoming that she may put herself down before someone else does, which could be seen as self-destructive behavior of some sort. This may be an issue in Jane's life, and it should be considered during the session. How do you consider it? Ask your client. When the client is comfortable, he or she may volunteer the information. If you have made good contact, you could mention that this is sometimes a trait in people when they feel very unsure of themselves, and did this ever happen when she was younger? Often, a person will respond, "Not only did I do it when I was younger, but I *still* do it." And then the situation can be counseled in depth.

Jane's Cancer Sun is symbolic of someone who may be easily inflamed emotionally, she may have a short emotional fuse. The traditional Capricorn Moon is squared by Saturn, and the Leo persona (ascendant) squares Uranus. The Uranus aspect to the ascendant can be read in key words as "I behave (Uranus) like a Taurus (Taurus characteristics) against the needs and best interests of my new beginnings (the ascendant)." Jane can be quite dynamic on the one hand, and very hard on herself on the other. If she doesn't think about what she's doing, the Taurus characteristics of being stubborn, self-centered, overly sensual, or grasping can be manifesting instead of the better Taurus energy that includes being practical, realistic, solid, and stable. The Taurus traits don't work easily with those of Leo (practicality versus idealism), and some inner conflicts will undoubtedly take place during her lifetime. She may do a number of things that are actually embarrassing to her image (persona).

To round out the picture, Mars in Scorpio trines the Sun. She can do a great deal of research, but she may not be using her energy that way. Mars signifies how she acts out her Sun. Both the Sun and Mars are in water signs, and water tends to operate by osmosis, so the action Jane takes may not look like the action that someone would take if Mars were in Aries for example. She may also get caught up in taking action to "get" someone, for Scorpio can be a vindictive sign. The only time she gets going may be when she's angry, or she may spend a lot of time "getting back at" important people in her life. With a Leo ascendant, getting back at someone she loves may also involve hurting herself. This will have to be discussed with her.

Because Mars trines her Sun, she can express her "I am" energy with ease. Mars in Scorpio isn't really an aggressive Mars, but it can be well used for some organizational purpose. She may be really good at management, working with a group to get at the facts, or working with a group that benefits humanity. Mars also signifies the sex drive, and she may be insecure sexually, needing more sexual attention than most people, or she may have had a number of lovers at times when she felt insecure.

For those who allow ten degree orbs, note the opposition between Mars at 23° Scorpio and Uranus at 13° Taurus. This is a large orb, but I would want to see if the energy is operating in the chart. Some compromise would have to be made between the way she acts (Mars) and the way she behaves (Uranus). Is she a bit of a bully? Is she hyperactive? Does she "behave" one way and actually "act out" differently? Does she go off half-cocked, taking ill-thought-out action when angry? When she is angry (if this aspect is working in the chart) is she self-destructive? Does she manifest action outwardly or does she do things to herself that ultimately hurt her more than she can hurt anyone else? When this aspect is considered in relation to the Sun/Pluto conjunction, how will she express this energy?

Both Scorpio and Cancer planets (as a matter of fact, all water signs) indicate some kind of emotional rejection at some level. I would have to talk with her about feelings of unwantedness, or whether she felt rejected as a child. I would wonder if feelings of that type would color her grownup relationships, and whether counseling could put some of that part of her life back into balance.

Venus in Gemini symbolizes how Jane thinks about all forms of loving. It's her intellectual concept of what love means to her, how she appreciates beauty; and in the mental sign of Gemini, she will try to intellectualize her emotions. This is kind of an interesting setup (it happens quite often in charts) and it creates an interesting dilemma. A Cancerian person wants to be loved personally, and Cancer is one of the most sensitive and emotional of the signs. Venus in Gemini is impersonal about love, and will talk about it more than it wants to do it. In order to develop completely as an individual, the qualities of the Gemini Venus must be integrated into the personality, but the integration will not be easy. When we love another person and that person can't give us what we need we can always leave; but what do we do when the dilemma takes place inside ourselves?

Jane has two important aspects influencing her Venus. She has Neptune square it and the South Node conjunct it. When Neptune aspects a personal planet it clouds issues, providing delusion or illusion about that facet of personality represented by the planet in the aspect. So everything she considers beautiful (Venus) will be affected by Neptune, including what her concept of love is. This will have a definite effect on her relationships, for she may be too idealistic about love, looking for an incredibly perfect relationship. This means she may be quite disappointed with her love life or with the people she loves.

To some astrologers, the nodal axis is very important. The North Node usually symbolizes our opportunities in life, and the South Node symbolizes what will happen if we don't use our opportunities well. If a personal planet is conjunct the South Node, this planet takes on new color, for the planet can be considered as symbolizing something karmic. For those people who contemplate the concept of karma in the chart, this aspect would indicate that love relationships, and how Jane looks at love, will be a major issue for her. This could be discussed in the session. Not with fear and terror, but with understanding. Neptune blinds us wherever it sits, and when it aspects Venus, we know that it will cloud issues of love. This can be worked with consciously if the client is told how the energy works. Learning to become as realistic as this aspect will allow can help Jane handle her relationships better, and she can become happier with her life. Note the sextile between Venus and Mercury: if she works with understanding her Venusian traits, she will be able to communicate better.

Jane's Background

After looking at the natal chart on page 140, you may find it interesting to hear about the person who actually came to see me. Jane was a fairly large woman, tall and big-boned. She wasn't overweight, but being big-boned and tall created an image of ungainliness. She obviously wasn't comfortable with her height because she slouched. An astrologer could see the influence of Pluto conjunct the Sun; she had a certain Plutonian intensity radiating out of her, but she wasn't using this energy as much as it was using her. It was almost as though the Pluto energy was driving her, and she was trying vainly to keep up with it. She was quite shy and didn't expect much from anyone, and I could see that she didn't expect much from me either. Coming to an astrologer was a sort of last-ditch attempt for her.

Jane had called me for an appointment from her hospital bed shortly after undergoing extensive surgery; a friend told her to call, and she did it immediately. The data for her birth chart wasn't accurate since she only had her mother's memory to rely upon. She wasn't born in this country, and a subsequent search turned up the fact that her birth time wasn't entered on her birth certificate. She went to a rectification specialist and had the chart rectified; the chart you see here is the rectified one. However, after the rectification work was done, Jane discovered a baby book and her birth time was actually recorded there as a few mintues later than the chart shown here.

Jane was born into an upper crust family and grew up being cared for by servants. Her parents traveled extensively, and she traveled with them when she was a child. She spoke several languages fluently, having learned them while traveling: she had lived in several large cities including London, Paris, Rome, and New York while her father pursued his business interests. She said she was a very lonely child, remembering bad times with servants who were not particularly nice to her. She felt abandoned by her parents, especially when she was mistreated by the servants. Her most secure years were spent in a private school and in college because the regimen and the group consciousness of fellow students provided the illusion of belonging to a family. She married shortly after getting her degree, and kept to her family tradition by marrying a man who was involved in major financial pursuits and who traveled a great deal.

She tried to create with her marriage the family she didn't have. She wanted children, security, and to be loved. Her husband was English by birth; she described him as a traditional type, cold and unemotional. She wasn't sure that he really loved *her* since her parents had provided a very healthy dowry when she married him; she wasn't sure whether he liked her or the money better.

Shorty after she married, her father died, and the companion-ship they had begun to develop as she got older was suddenly gone. She was not close to her mother, didn't care for her at all, found her mother to be cold and withdrawn, unfeeling, unemotional. Jane wanted a close-knit family; and because she had few relatives and had been an only child, she wanted to have a large family. She did: two boys and two girls. She lavished all her bottled-up love on her children, and admitted to being a smother lover, which eventually alienated the children. One child left home early and another became a juvenile delinquent, much to the embarrassment of her husband. She spent a great deal of time chasing the illusion of the happy family, with Christmas at Grandmother's and that sort of thing. It didn't work for her. This was a big issue with her.

Jane's husband traveled a great deal, leaving her to raise the kids. She didn't want to travel with him as she didn't enjoy her own early childhood travels. (Students should note Jane's retrograde Saturn in the 9th house, which usually indicates a person who doesn't feel comfortable traveling in strange places.) Jane didn't want a lot of servants because of her own early childhood experience with them, so she tried to maintain a huge home by herself. She was housekeeper, house manager, den mother, children's chauffeur, and caterer for her husband's business dinners when necessary. Busy as she was, she was bored and lonely. She said that her social group consisted of her husband's friends and business contacts. Everything they did was phoney—the lovely gourmet dinners, the country club—and she couldn't find a spot for her own personality or the development of her interests in the midst of that lifestyle.

Her husband didn't want her to take a job but she did manage to become involved in some large community projects doing volunteer work. This helped her to learn something about her management ability, and she discovered that she liked to think. She felt even more frustrated at that point because she couldn't really do anything with her energy because the children were still too small to leave alone. She also admitted that she didn't want to leave the children alone for fear they would feel unwanted as she had when she was a child.

She had no close friends, and especially no women friends in whom she could confide. She tried some psychotherapy but didn't like it. She also dabbled in a few neighborhood groups but didn't find what she was looking for. It could be that she couldn't verbalize what she was looking for, so no one could help her.

In her search for herself, she chose to pursue the worst of the late thirties patterns, and began to drink too much. She was feeling very insecure at the time; her husband wasn't paying attention to her, so she sought security and attention from other men. She had an affair but didn't really like it. The worst part of the affair was that her husband didn't catch her; it was too easy for her to have it. So she decided to get his attention by having an affair with her gardener, who was an ex-alcoholic, ex-drug-abuser, had a jail record, and was on probation. She flaunted this relationship in the neighborhood and finally her husband found out. Instead of getting the attention she was looking for—an emotional outburst, anger, or maybe hurt feelings—her husband was quietly stunned. As far as he was concerned, he couldn't understand how his wife could sink to this, and asked for a divorce. A bitter custody fight ensued and a divorce eventually took place.

She didn't handle the divorce very well. Jane was really looking for some attention. The gardener seemed to appreciate her as a woman, and she hadn't felt like one for some time. She thought her husband would be upset, but she didn't think he would want a divorce: she certainly didn't. He wanted to take the children from her. She was so shocked at her husband's response that she got a second-rate lawyer who didn't represent her very well. She didn't get a good custody agreement for the children, nor decent child support, nor decent alimony. The dowry she brought into the marriage wasn't mentioned in court and the joint property wasn't settled very well. She got the house, but it carried a large mortage. The house was essentially a white elephant, and although it was worth a great deal on paper, it wasn't easy to sell. So the money she might get someday wasn't forthcoming. The child support payments were inadequate, as was her alimony, considering the family income and considering her background.

Jane began to wonder if her whole marriage had been a hoax, as her husband remarried very shortly after the divorce was settled. This made her think that he must have married her for the family money, and the thought made her even more depressed. She was in the middle of midlife crisis, she didn't know who she was or where she was going; she didn't see the gardener anymore for that relationship paled when the divorce took place. She didn't have a marriage prospect for herself, and didn't like dealing with her husband's new wife, which was necessary because of the children's visitation rights.

When she came to me for the reading, she had fallen apart and was very ill. She was in the process of trying to sell her house because she couldn't afford to live there any longer. She would have to move, take the children from private schools, and start a completely new life. And to top it off, her son had been arrested for stealing a car. Her mother did offer to help: Jane could have moved back into New York City and Mom would have paid the bills, but Jane would have lost all her freedom. The children would be under the grandmother's thumb and this was not a viable solution for her.

JANE'S TRANSITS

The first reading was done in April, 1978, and the transits we will discuss now are calculated for that time. When I work with transits,

I work from Pluto back to Mars because I like to see what the slower moving planets are doing. The generation planets (Pluto, Neptune, and Uranus) reflect the mood of the chart for me, while the maturation planets (Saturn, Jupiter, and Mars) show activity involving the conscious maturation process of the moment.[5]

Pluto by transit is at 14° Libra 56′ ℞, and is not ready to cycle into the Pluto square Pluto phase, as natal Pluto is at 28° Cancer 18′. But Pluto by transit is beginning to affect natal Jupiter at 21° Capricorn 39′ ℞ in the 6th house. Because Jupiter opposes the Sun-Pluto natal conjunction in the chart, an insidious unseating of confidence is beginning to take place.

Neptune by transit is at 18° Sagittarius 05′ ℞, while natal Neptune is at 16° Virgo 56′. Neptune has already made its first square in the first cycle to itself, probably bringing with it some loss of an ideal—some dream has been dissolved or some fantasy about reality has been exposed to the light of day in an unattractive way. Natal Neptune is in the 2nd house, indicating some delusion about income, or even a delusion about personal worth or security. Zip Dobyns said many years ago that the 2nd house indicates possessions—money and the possessions that you own, but also your talents, for talents are possessions in a sense. The Neptune square would come from the 5th house, indicating the possibility of some delusion regarding love life or children, and the square would bring a change of some kind. The side issue here might be one that would affect matters related to concepts or ideals about 2nd and 5th house matters. The main issue is that some idealistic goal in life needs to change.

Uranus by transit is at 15° Scorpio 02′, and has already passed the opposition to itself; Jane's natal Uranus is at 13° Taurus 20′. Going back in the ephemeris, you will note that Uranus went into a ten-degree applying orb to natal Uranus on November 4, 1975, staying there until June 14, 1976. It retrograded out of orb, and returned August 7, 1976, staying until November 24, 1977. Looking ahead in the ephemeris, you will discover the cycle is still not finished at the time the reading was done, as Uranus will retrograde back to 13° Taurus 20′ on May 31, 1978, and will remain in orb until September 8, 1978. Then she is done with that aspect.

For those who use large orbs, please note the ten-degree opposition in the natal chart between Mars and Uranus. If such a

---

[5] For a more detailed description of transits see my book *Transits: The Time of Your Life*. Samuel Weiser, Inc., York Beach, ME, 1980.

large natal orb is allowed, then the Uranus aspect would remain active until October 1, 1980. Please note also that Jane's ascendant is 11° Leo as is her Mercury, and the natal square between Uranus and Mercury/ascendant will start this aspect working even earlier, as it will bring energy to the chart when transiting Uranus comes into orb with the ascendant and Mercury.

Saturn by transit is at 23° Leo and her ascendant is 11° Leo. That means she has already gone through some major change in lifestyle. I don't know what kind of change will have taken place, but I will discuss it when I see her. She's not in the middle of any Saturn aspect at the moment, nor is she dealing with a Saturn cycle.

Jupiter is transiting at 1° Cancer 07° and her natal Jupiter is at 21° Capricorn 39' R. She started her last Jupiter cycle between December 2, 1972 and January 17, 1973, at age thirty-six. Jupiter will move to the opposition in the fourth cycle between June 10th and July 28, 1978. Because natal Jupiter opposes the Sun-Pluto conjunction at 28° Cancer, the opposition will really be in effect until August 30, 1978.

When preparing to see a client, I usually provide a list of Mars transits and cycles. In some cases, beginning to work with Mars cycles provides some time sequences (of short duration) that allow plans to be made in the process of moving ahead in life. The Mars cycles can give a sense of goal orientation to people who have not been previously successful at directing themselves. I usually go back to the last cycle to see when it began, for sometimes the client remembers what happened. We then work ahead for a year or so, using both the transits and cycles. Because Mars is a two to two and a half year cycle, I usually go through at least one complete cycle, providing the dates for decision making in case the client doesn't return.

Natal Mars is at 23° Scorpio and it is direct. In April, 1978, Mars by transit was at 3° Leo. Her last Mars cycle had begun between October 28 and November 11, 1976. The first square took place between February 26 and March 11, 1977. The opposition hit June 24 through July 8, 1977, and the last square in that cycle will take place May 12 through June 1, 1978. At the last square she will have to clean up something related to the decision she made in November, 1976. She will start a new Mars cycle between October 9 and October 23, 1978, so I will ask her to pay attention to what she is thinking about in regard to either a love situation (relationship) or a job opportunity. The decision she makes in October, 1978, will have to be adjusted between February 6 and February 19, 1979, and when the opposition occurs (between June 3 and June 17, 1979) she will know whether or not her plan is working.

JANE'S CYCLES

To review the transits, which really give you the key to a client's cycles, we'll discuss them briefly again. Pluto is causing some kind of unseating influence, but Jane is not in the midst of a Pluto cycle. She has already experienced the first square in the Neptune cycle, and I would discuss that in retrospect to see how the energy has affected her lifestyle. Uranus is not in orb at the moment, but it will return, so essentially the midlife crisis symbolized by the Uranus opposition to itself is still very much active. This will be a session devoted to midlife crisis counseling. Saturn is not active cyclically. A Jupiter phase (the opposition in the fourth cycle) is coming up and the fourth cycle needs to be explained. We will discuss her Mars cycles whether they are active or not in order to prepare her for using Mars energy to her best advantage.

THE SESSION

The format you choose when you work with a client may vary from the one that follows. I always try to begin at the beginning and proceed to a conclusion! As I mentioned at the beginning of this section, I like to start talking about the natal chart, and work up to transits, ending with the cycles. But that doesn't always work, as some sessions end up being very different than I planned. If my client is somewhat comfortable about our meeting, I try to open up the session by explaining the value to be gained from understanding the symbolism provided by astrology. Then I try to discuss some of the facets of the natal chart, hoping that the client will begin to see some familiar patterns. Planets and aspects can be explained in terms of various strengths and energies available, being assets when they are understood and stumbling blocks when they are not. When the chart is viewed as a "map" of personal needs and values, this part of the session can move along quite easily. And a client who has spent some time doing self-evaluation is usually more responsive than one who has not.

Sometimes I start a session with the transits and cycles, and begin to explain natal configurations according to which ones are currently activated by the transiting energy. This sometimes works, especially when the person insists on viewing the astrologer as a psychic. Some clients completely take over a session by blurting out whatever needs to be blurted out, and you have to pick up the pieces they leave scattered all over your rug. Each person will respond differently, and we learn to adjust to the client's needs. It doesn't matter which way you work; it *does* matter that the client gets a chance to have some input into the session.

If you are just beginning to work with clients, you'll notice that your style will drastically change after doing your first fifty readings. You'll become less insecure and more willing to let the client communicate. My biggest problem when I first began to read was that I tried to tell the client everything I knew. "See how much I know?" The poor person didn't get a chance to get a word in edgewise, and when someone did manage to outtalk me, I felt guilty because I didn't think I had said enough to earn my money. It never dawned on me that the client might need to talk, or that the client had absorbed enough information for one day. I exhausted us both! No matter what other astrologers may tell you to the contrary, none of us are good readers when we begin.

Astrologers also serve another function that many don't understand. We're so busy trying to be accepted as legitimate professionals that we don't understand that not being legitimate has its value. People who go to an astrologer often feel more free to talk than they would if the conversation were directed at a "real" therapist or ministerial figure. People talk to me when they won't, or can't, talk to anyone else. I learned how to listen; my clients have taught me a great deal about the nuances of the aspects.

Every now and then you may get a client who thinks you're a psychic or a fortune teller. These people put a lot of power on astrologers—power that we don't have. If that happens, I try to dispel that imagery really fast, and one of the best ways to do that is to start asking questions about natal aspects.

Jane was looking for a psychic and a confessor when she came to me. She needed to talk about what was happening with her, and that was okay with me. She was also looking for me to be someone who would tell her if she would die or not, and I had to tell her that I didn't have that kind of power. Only she and her God could make any headway on that issue. Once she discovered I was not psychic, we could begin to talk, and we talked about the potential of her natal chart at the very beginning of the session.

Because we weren't certain of Jane's birth time at the first session, I had to work quite carefully. The conversation went something like this: "Each person has a birth chart, and we don't know whether the chart we are working with today is exactly right because your birth data is a little uncertain. But I'm going to talk to you about your natal aspects because they should be in effect no matter what time of the day you were born. There are other astrological factors [the houses] we can discuss better when we get your data confirmed." Some astrologers would say that I should not have done the reading because I didn't have her time of birth. However, this was a woman who wanted a reading very badly; she was ill, she didn't know if she would survive, and she didn't have time to wait as far as she was concerned. We would all like to wait for the perfect time to read someone's chart, but life doesn't always give us that much leeway.

We discussed the possibilities of personality based on Jane's Cancer Sun, Capricorn Moon, and maybe Leo (maybe Virgo) rising. I approached her aspects with questions, and asked if she felt or related to any of the things that I discussed with her. Jane had a terrible problem knowing who she was. One could say, "Well, so does everybody," and I would agree. But when that question is asked in a session, it has to be asked carefully. Using key words, talking about circumstances, asking the client for circumstances that have caused discomfort in the past will all help to bring the issue to some kind of a head. Jane never fit in with her peers. She was bigger than everyone else, and she thought differently than the other children she knew. Astrologers know that other children born the same year Jane was also have Pluto conjunct the Sun. But if Jane didn't meet anyone born around that time of year, she might not know anyone who had it, or she might not be able to talk about it. She was quite intuitive, and some of her psychic experiences had caused her a great deal of apprehension when she was younger. She also had a great deal of pain about the Cancer/Capricorn Sun-Moon expression of herself because her innards were always at war. She lit up when we talked about the Jupiter-Sun opposition and the Moon-Saturn square because she related to that all over the place. Taking charge of herself by understanding the various components of her personality was an exciting idea for her, and we decided to take this further in another session.

Midlife crisis was the basis for the time we spent together. I talked about the Pluto transit and the possibility of feelings of insecurity gradually developing. She had felt this energy in addition to the helplessness she felt with midlife crisis. We talked about the Neptune disillusionment at the first Neptune square, and out came the marriage problems, the gardener, and the stupid divorce settlement. She told me that she was so stunned by the divorce that she never told her lawyer about the dowry and the money she had brought into the marriage, so the court scene was played as though she were entirely taken care of by her husband's income. In the midst of the divorce discussion we had to see when the divorce had taken place. Of course it happened when Saturn crossed the Sun-Pluto conjunction, and the divorce went through when Saturn crossed the ascendant. (We confirmed this once the chart had been rectified.) The change in lifestyle was inevitable because something has to change when Saturn crosses the ascendant, but it doesn't have to be bad. In reminiscing about her marriage, she talked about her husband, and began to realize that she didn't know him very well. She softened up considerably when we began to look at her Neptune square Venus. She seemed to want to work on the idea that the man might not have been as bad as he seemed.

The most important thing that Jane got out of the first session was that she was not the only person undergoing crisis at her age. We discussed the possibility of death, and it relieved her that it didn't bother me to talk about it with her. I didn't avoid the issue, I asked her what she thought about it. It had bothered everyone else she had tried to discuss it with. We also talked about the fact that everyone goes through insecurities at midlife as I explained the Uranus-Uranus opposition to her. She loved it. She felt much better. She decided she could manage to take a look at her life. Remember the five cardinal planets and the four earth? These indicators let you know that here is a woman who will do something if someone exposes her to an idea. A person like Jane didn't need someone to take care of her, she needed new insight into herself so that she could begin to take care of herself in a new way—actually to let herself *be* herself. This can be quite an exciting proposition.

Jane didn't feel that she had handled the beginning of her fourth Jupiter cycle very well, and she found the dates of that cycle interesting in terms of what she was doing. She was dismayed to learn that an astrologer who didn't know her could talk to her about the cycle and actually describe her behavior. She was dismayed that the "typical" late thirties insecurity that tied to the Jupiter cycle was what she was feeling. She didn't know that this happened to other women. She felt that if she had known more about the possibilities of this cycle, she would have been able to handle the energy differently, and maybe she could have avoided some of the personal traumas she experienced, or maybe she could have worked out her problems another way. She wanted to work with the cycle, and since the opposition would occur that summer, she would have some time to try to work with the energy. Because her marriage was over, she decided that the best thing to do would be to get on with teaching her children what they needed to learn, and would try to work out some of the problems with them. (When a client responds with dismay to something that has already taken place, it becomes necessary to counsel the futility of "crying over spilt milk." We can only go ahead, and the client needs to hear that.)

Jane was well pleased with the idea of working with Mars cycles and transits. She wanted to begin to time some of her plans which would tie into the Mars work cycle. We had discussed her anger previously (the Mars-Uranus and Uranus-ascendant aspects) and she thought that using the Mars transits would help her alleviate some of the pain she created for herself.

The first session started a series of visits. I saw Jane once a month for about six months, and I used her chart in this book because she taught me a great deal about how astrology can be used in the counseling process. Jane basically did her own counseling: my role was to make sure that she kept her perspective as she explored herself. For six months Jane took her chart apart. She came in with lists of questions about behavior, personal needs, and situations she wanted to clarify. She sent me lists of questions that involved dates from her past, so I could prepare for the session ahead of time. She wanted to explore important times and themes in her life. She probed to understand herself, and was extremely open once she started this journey. We met and shared tears and laughter while she was finding her way, and I was privileged to learn with her.

The issues that were handled during those six months were her obsession about her children, the similarity in the terminology she used to describe her mother and her husband, her fear of not being loved. After she became more comfortable with looking at herself, she realized that it was time to explore renegotiating the divorce settlement as it pertained to her children, and she made plans to handle that part of her life.

Jane wanted me to be her therapist and I couldn't accept that responsibility. I was willing to help her understand her natal chart, but I wasn't willing to be her sole contact with herself. She didn't know where to go to get further counseling, so I recommended a number of places for her to try, giving her enough choices so she could select something that interested her. She also attended seminars and participated in group activities that related to healing, self-help, and spiritual development. During the following year, she took a class in Religious Science, a course in herbology, became a vegetarian, took a Kübler-Ross seminar on death and dying, joined a single mothers group in her neighborhood for counseling about being a single parent, studied wicca for the earth ritual of it, worked with full-moon meditations, explored the Bach flower remedies, and essentially opened up her world. Her new contacts accomplished several things for her: she started to meet people she liked; she was able to accept or reject ideas as she responded to them personally; she established a broader base so she did not need to depend on me.

During this six month counseling period, Jane began to stand taller, dress differently (she said she had to get her corporate image together), and became obviously more self-assured. She began to accept herself. She began to realize that other people liked her.

Thank you, Jane, for becoming you.

MORE CYCLES

Some readers may be interested in some other astrological cycles, and it might be a nice idea to go back in history for a minute to discuss how other astrologers used planetary cycles. Before doing so we should bear in mind a few basics about old astrology books. Most astrologers were involved with some form of spiritual development, most had strong religious ideas, and most related planetary configurations to a grand universal plan of evolving consciousness. Until recently, most people have not had the luxury of being able to explore themselves from an analytical point of view, and the older texts reflect that fact. Today, all too many students say they don't want to read the older books because they are so "negative," or they don't apply to today's interest in astrology. They do, but you have to read between the lines. All modern astrologers have studied astrology with someone, and contemporary astrologers have essentially retranslated the astrological interpretations of yesteryear into terminology that can be more easily understood today.

Most of the early books are concerned with progressions and horary questions. You will notice that a mere twenty pages or so is assigned to the calculation and interpretation of natal planets and aspects, and the birth chart itself, and we are quickly moved to progressions and information pertaining to horary questions. Not enough time spent on the basics, we moderns say. But the older astrologer was basically answering questions for clients. People were concerned with survival in those days. Today a client wants to know his or her inner motivations. Just one hundred years ago, people were not concerned with finding a meaningful career, they were concerned with finding work. Any kind. Food and a roof over your head was a big issue. Today we have unemployment and medicaid, and in a pinch a government agency may take care of our needs. This means that the questions a client asks an astrologer will be different.

So when you read the old books you'll see a lot of questions that don't confront us today. Questions such as, "Will my baby live? Will my wife or daughter live through childbirth? Will I get to keep my child?" Life was a big issue then, and even keeping a baby was an issue, for when there was no money, babies were given away or even sold because the parents couldn't afford to keep them. Yet in between the lines of these old books can be found gems that can be updated to the terms we use today.

There are many theories to the planetary cycles that were used in the old days. These cycles are still used today in some countries, and you may enjoy trying themself. Sepharial considered the planetary cycles in relation to the Hindu system of the yugas, and relates these cycles to 120 year increments.[1] Students interested in studying Hindu astrology may enjoy working with some of his theories, or they may even prove that they don't work. I don't know because I don't have any experience with the Hindu system.

The most common thing to do was to assign a certain amount of years of life to a particular planet. When you read a chart, you would compare the client's age with the cycle he was ruled by, and then check the ruling planet in the natal chart. Predictions could be made based on the natal aspects and the house placement of the planet, especially when this information was synthesized with the question posed by the client. Some years ago I chanced on a copy of Raphael's private lessons, written in 1903. He recommended Ptolemy's cycles, which assigned the following planetary rulerships to different phases of life.

Age 0-4: The Moon (ruling for 4 years)
Age 4-14: Mercury (ruling for 10 years)
Age 14-22: Venus (ruling for 8 years)
Age 22-41: The Sun (ruling for 19 years)
Age 41-56: Mars (ruling for 15 years)
Age 56-68: Jupiter (ruling for 12 years)
Age 68 through the end of life: Saturn (no years listed)

Raphael recorded in his lesson plan that he would alter this schema somewhat, as he found from his experience that he would prefer to change the rulerships as follows:

---

[1]Sepharial, *Cosmic Symbolism*, William Rider & Son, Ltd., London, 1912. See Chapter 10.

Moon: Age 0-4
Mercury: Age 4-14
Venus: Age 14-24
Sun: Age 24-40
Mars: Age 40-50
Jupiter: Age 50-60
Saturn and Uranus: The rest of life

His disagreement with Ptolemy basically concerned the Jupiter phase, as "after age 60, the years become so fatal that it seems incorrect for Jupiter to hold sway." He worked with the cyclic planetary rulerships because "the general fortune of the native during these respective ages will depend in great measure on the position and power of the planet ruling that period. Thus, if Venus is very strong, well-placed and unafflicted, it would show that the general fortune of the native from age 14 to 24 or 25 years would be good; if the Sun, Mars or any of the other planets were similarly placed, it would show that success would predominate at such a period. On the contrary, a weak and afflicted planet would denote many troubles and misfortunes at its period of life, according to how, and where it is placed If in the 10th, the credit or business would suffer; if in the 8th deaths and bereavements; in the 2nd loss of money; in the 5th loss or worry through children, and so on with the other houses."[2]

In his book *Transits and Planetary Periods,* Sepharial mentions the Chaldean system, and links the following planetary rulership for phases of life:[3]

Moon: 4 years
Mercury: 10 years
Venus: 8 years
Sun: 19 years
Mars: 15 years
Jupiter: 12 years
Saturn: 30 years

Working up into the more modern material, Margaret Hone has a nice little discussion of the Shakespearian reference to the

[2]*Raphael's Private Instructions in Genethliacal Astrology* (revised and amended), London 1903, self-published. It is interesting to note that the book is actually handwritten, and contains Raphael's natal chart, whereupon he admits to being the second Raphael. It was evidently a course handbook for his students.

[3]Sepharial, *Transits and Planetary Periods,* Samuel Weiser, Inc., York Beach, ME, 1970. See Chapter 1. Originally published in London in 1920.

seven ages of life in *As You Like It,* and here she is relating the cycles to the seven stages symbolized by the seven planets. She comments that the end of life so sarcastically expressed by Shakespeare would better be symbolized by the newly discovered planet Neptune.[4]

> ...At first the infant
> Mewling and puking in the nurses ' arms;
> And then the whining schoolboy with his satchel
> And shining morning face, creeping, like a snail,
> Unwillingly to school. And then the lover
> Sighing like a furnace, with a woeful ballad
> Made to his mistress' eyebrow. Then a soldier
> Full of strange oaths, and bearded like the pard,
> Jealous in honour, sudden and quick to quarrel,
> Seeking the bubble reputation
> Even in the cannon's mouth. And then the justice
> In fair round belly with good capon lined
> With eyes severe and beard of formal cut,
> Full of wise saws and modern instances
> And so he plays his part. The sixth age shifts
> Into the lean and slippered pantaloon
> With spectacles on nose and pouch on side
> His youthful hose, well sav'd a world too wide
> For his shrunk shank; and his big manly voice
> Turning again toward childish treble, pipes
> And whistles in his sound. Last scene of all
> That ends this strange eventful history,
> In second childishness, and mere oblivion
> Sans teeth, sans eyes, sans taste, sans everything.

She feels that we go from babe, to student, lover, soldier, to justice and then death with Moon, Mercury, Venus, Mars, Jupiter, and Saturn being discussed. I wonder if this could be interpreted differently: for Moon rules the babe, Mercury rules the student, Venus rules the lover, Mars rules the warrior, but Justice doesn't have to be Jupiter in this case, as the "wise saws and severe eyes" might be relating to the Sun's position at the height of its glory. Moving on to Jupiter, with spectacles and early youth gone, the blustering man is no longer in sight, and this seems to me when Jupiter would be able to express itself in terms of philosophy. Of

---

[4]Hone, *The Modern Textbook of Astrology,* Fowler & Co., Ltd., London, 1951, pp. 30-32.

course the end comes without teeth and hearing, and Saturn is the Grim Reaper. Interesting to note also that the Moon begins life and Saturn ends it—both Moon and Saturn phases being without teeth!

Recently I heard Doris Hebel giving a lecture (actually at the NASO conference in Washington, D. C., in 1983) where she was talking about the following planetary rulerships:

Moon: Age 0-6
Mercury: Age 7-13
Venus: Age 14-20
Sun: Age 21-27
Mars: Age 28-34
Jupiter: Age 35-41
Saturn: Age 42-48
Uranus: Age 49-55
Neptune: Age 56-63
Pluto: Age 64-70

After her lecture I asked where that system came from because it was a little different from the ones I had read about. She said that she had heard Julie Baum (AFA) lecture on the subject in the mid-1960s and hopes that she remembers the material correctly. Baum learned this system from German astrologers, who are evidently using it today. One of the points Hebel made was that when the Pluto rulership ends, you start all over again, with a new Moon cycle, and repeat the pattern. Hebel said that perhaps this was some kind of an evolutionary pattern, where planetary rulerships change and extend based on the discovery of new planetary bodies. Prior to the discovery of Pluto, for instance, the average American life span was about 62 or 63. Now it has increased to about 70. In future years it may increase even more.

Thinking about what Hebel said, and going back to Rudhyar's concepts in *Planetary Aspects,* it's interesting to consider that as we continue to age, we will have more chance of experiencing all phases of consciousness without the biproduct of senility. A few short years ago, many of our older people were relegated out of the work world and retired. Now our seniors are fighting for·independence, even in nursing homes. As we have more options to deal with this new consciousness, who knows what will happen?